Meatless Eats

Meatless Eats

Savory Vegetarian Dishes from
Around the World

Instructables.com
Edited by Sarah James

Skyhorse Publishing

Skyhorse Publishing books may be purchased in bulk at special discounts for sales promotion, corporate gifts, fund-raising, or educational purposes. Special editions can also be created to specifications. For details, contact the Special Sales Department, Skyhorse Publishing, 307 West 36th Street, 11th Floor, New York, NY 10018 or info@skyhorsepublishing.com.

Skyhorse® and Skyhorse Publishing® are registered trademarks of Skyhorse Publishing, Inc.®, a Delaware corporation.

Visit our website at www.skyhorsepublishing.com.

10 9 8 7 6 5 4 3 2 1

Library of Congress Cataloging-in-Publication Data is available on file.

ISBN: 978-1-62087-697-8

Printed in China

Disclaimer:

This book is intended to offer general guidance. It is sold with the understanding that every effort was made to provide the most current and accurate information. However, errors and omissions are still possible. Any use or misuse of the information contained herein is solely the responsibility of the user, and the author and publisher make no warrantees or claims as to the truth or validity of the information. The author and publisher shall have neither liability nor responsibility to any person or entity with respect to any loss or damage caused, or alleged to have been caused, directly or indirectly, by the information contained in this book. Furthermore, this book is not intended to give professional dietary, technical, or medical advice. Please refer to and follow any local laws when using any of the information contained herein, and act responsibly and safely at all times.

Table of Contents

Introduction

Welcome to *Meatless Eats*. Here you'll find the kinds of vegetarian foods that should be fed to anyone who complains that "a meal without meat is not a meal." These are filling, flavorful, and simple dishes that anyone can put together. Each of these forty-two veggie recipes was created, photographed, and shared by talented and creative home cooks from Instructables.com.

These authors don't just tell you how they made the dish, they also tell the story of why they made it. Like the best hand-me-down cookbooks, these recipes are more than just an ingredient list accompanied by terse instructions. They're infused with the stories of real people who make food to feed themselves and their families.

It is my hope that you will riff on these recipes to create innovative dishes that you and your family will enjoy. Modify, adapt, iterate, remix, and make something for yourself and your family that makes everyone happy.

Section 1
Mediterranean

How to Prepare Scrumptious Caponata

By rupamagic
(http://www.instructables.com/
id/How-to-Prepare-Scrumptious-
Caponata/)

According to Wikipedia: Caponata is a Sicilian eggplant relish made from chopped fried vegetables (eggplants, peppers, celery, olives, etc.), seasoned sweet vinegar and served with capers in a bittersweet sauce. Variations of the ingredients exist: the "classical" recipes on the whole island number well over thirty-seven. It is a delicious and relatively simple dish to prepare, and it tastes great hot or cold. I find it tastes better the day after you make it, especially cold and served with fresh water-packed mozzarella and ciabatta bread.

Step 1: Gather the Goods

Ingredients

- 1 medium-large eggplant, cut into (approximately) 1-inch pieces
- ¼ cup olive oil
- 1 stalk of celery, chopped
- 1 red bell pepper, cut into ½-inch pieces (I use a mix of red/orange/yellow when available)
- 1 medium onion, chopped
- 1 (14-ounce) can diced tomatoes
- 3 tablespoons raisins
- ¼ cup red wine vinegar
- 2 tablespoon drained capers (you can use olives in place of or in addition to capers)
- 1 fat garlic clove, peeled and minced
- 2 teaspoons sugar
- ½ teaspoon dried oregano leaves
- Salt and pepper

Serving Suggestion Ingredients

- 1 loaf ciabatta bread or other delicious rustic bread
- Generous slices of fresh (water-packed) mozzarella

Step 2: Salt and Sweat the Eggplant

First cut up the eggplant and spread it out in a single layer over a clean flour cloth or a few layers of paper towel. Sprinkle it with salt all over (using about one rounded teaspoon to cover each eggplant), toss it around to coat all sides lightly, and spread evenly again in one layer. Then cover with another layer or two of towel. Let it "sweat" for at least 15 minutes. Don't worry, most of this salt will not go into the final dish.

Step 4: Mise en Place

Chefs on cooking shows make everything look so easy and fast! This is a large part of it. "Mise en place" is a French term meaning "everything in its place." Arranging a mise en place just means that you measure out all of your ingredients, chop, grate, or slice all veggies, etc., and arrange them in the order that they will be used or in a way that makes using them most convenient before you begin cooking. It's like having an assistant in the kitchen with you even when you are alone. This preparation makes your culinary experience much more smooth and pleasant and allows you to socialize more while cooking, which is always a joy.

Step 3: Dice, Chop, Measure, Etc.

Meanwhile, dice the onion and chop the celery and peppers to approximately ½-inch pieces. Measure out your other ingredients and set it all up (mise en place) while you wait for the eggplant to sweat.

Step 5: Wring out Water (and Salt) from Eggplant

Cover eggplant with more towels and press it down, then roll it up and squeeze out as much of the water and salt as you can. Don't be gentle—at this stage the eggplant is simply a sponge, and the less water it has in it the better t will plump up again and be saturated with deliciousness from all the other ingredients.

Step 6: Heat Oil

Once all your ingredients are laid out, heat the oil in a heavy large skillet over medium heat—be careful not to get it too hot, as olive oil scorches at a relatively low temperature.

Step 7: Add Celery

Add the celery to the hot oil and fry about 2 minutes.

Step 8: Add Onion and Eggplant

Add half the onion and the eggplant and fry about another 2 minutes. Season with salt (about ½ teaspoon should be fine for one eggplant) and fresh ground black pepper, if available.

mediterranean

Step 9: Add Bell Peppers

Add the bell peppers and cook about another 3 minutes.

Step 10: Add Remaining Onion

Add the remaining onion and cook until translucent (about 3 minutes).

Step 11: Add Tomatoes, Raisins, and Spice

Add the diced tomatoes with their juices, raisins, and oregano. Season again with salt and pepper to taste. Simmer over medium-low heat, stirring often, until the flavors blend and the mixture thickens (about 20 minutes).

Step 12: Final Flavoring

Add the vinegar, sugar, and capers (and/or olives). Season once more with salt and pepper if needed. Serve hot over pasta, as an open-faced warm sandwich over ciabatta bread or other toast, with fresh mozzarella if desired, or chilled the next day. I find this always tastes better the next day, especially chilled. Serves six as a main course, and ten as a side or starter.

Eggplant Parmesan

By randofo
(http://www.instructables.com/
id/Eggplant-Parmesan/)

- A couple of plates
- Oven-safe glass dish
- A colander
- Paper towels
- Bowls
- Cutting boards
- Utensils

Eggplant parmesan is a delightfully delicious vegetarian dish. Not only does it taste great, but it is easy to make. And who doesn't love Italian food? I mean, really, red sauce, cheese, and fried eggplant—how can you go wrong? This is, after all, one of my favorite dishes of all time. I hope that you enjoy it as much as I do.

Step 1: Ingredients and Equipment

Ingredients
- A large eggplant
- Large block of mozzarella cheese
- Romano pecorino (parmesan) cheese
- 2 eggs
- ¼ cup milk
- Parsley flakes
- Garlic powder
- Marinara sauce
- Italian-style bread crumbs
- Canola oil

Step 2: Cut the Eggplant

Slice the eggplant into slices between ½ inch and ¾ inch thick.

8

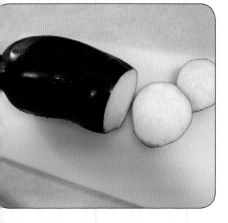

tep 3: Salt It

Sprinkle salt onto your hands and ghtly rub it into the surface of the ggplant slices. Let them sit for at ast 30 minutes in a colander. This will elp pull out the excess water from the ggplant and cut the acidity.

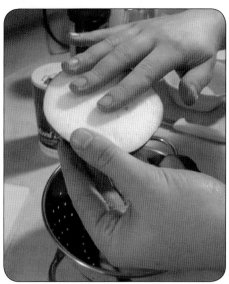

mediterranean

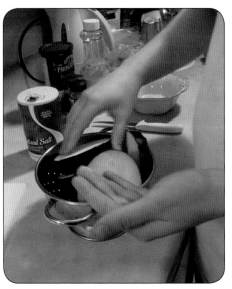

Step 4: Make Batter

Make the egg batter by mixing together an egg, ¼ cup of milk, a few sprinkles of garlic powder, and a generous amount of parsley flakes. After you mix it well, if there does not appear to be any parsley flakes floating on top of the surface, sprinkle some more into the mix.

Step 6: Batter Up

Battering the eggplant is actually quite easy. All you need to do is pick up an eggplant slice and then dunk it into the egg mixture until all sides are covered. Let the excess batter drip off the eggplant and then dredge it through the bread crumbs until it is completely covered in crumbs. This should happen relatively quickly and not take a lot of work. Place the breaded eggplants in a pile on a plate.

Step 5: Bread Crumbs

I swear by Progresso Italian-style bread crumbs. In other projects in which I have used these, people have suggested making your own breadcrumbs with lightly stale bread and a little bit of Romano pecorino (parmesan) cheese. Feel free to give this a try.

mediterranean

Step 8: Fry It

Carefully place the eggplant into the frying pan with a fork. Let it cook for 2 to 3 minutes, and then flip all the slices over so that the other sides can cook for the same amount of time. Repeat flipping the eggplant over until it is evenly brown on each side. If you can stick a fork through without resistance and both sides are browned, it's done. Place the fried eggplant on a clean plate with a paper towel on it to absorb the oil. Place another paper towel over top to absorb the oil on both sides.

Tip: Later, should you be inclined, you can cook off even more of the oil by baking it in the preheated oven for 2 to 3 minutes before you add the sauce and cheese.

Step 7: Prepare for Frying

Fill your frying pan with enough oil that, when you place it in, the eggplant will be half-submerged. Heat the oil on a medium to high flame.

Step 9: Cut the Cheese

Slice your block of mozzarella cheese into long slices that are about ¼ inch thick. Tip: I advise against using fresh mozzarella balls, as they tend to be too watery and typically not salty enough to cut the sweetness of the sauce.

13

Step 10: Saucy

Pour your sauce into the pan such that the eggplant will be half-submerged. Flip the eggplant over a few times until it is fully covered in sauce.

Step 11: Put It All Together

Sprinkle on Romano pecorino (parmesan) cheese. Distribute your pre sliced mozzarella cheese over top of the eggplant slices.

Step 12: Bake

Preheat the oven to 325°F and then bake the eggplant until the pieces of cheese start to melt together and bubble. This should take about 5 to 10 minutes to happen. Once it does, take it out and serve.

15

mediterranean

Vegan Bolognese Sauce

By scoochmaroo
(http://www.instructables.com/id/Vegan-Bolognese-Sauce/)

This scrumptious sauce is a vegan take on the classic Bolognese recipe. I dare you to try it and not fall in love with its hearty, smoky flavor! The addition of smoked tempeh replaces the texture of hamburger and the flavor of the pancetta or bacon, while roasted eggplant adds a deep richness.

Bolognese sauce is traditionally a meat- and pork- based sauce. I had a desire to lighten up this dish by making it all vegetarian. In fact, it's easy enough to make vegan—thereby creating delicious, stick-to-your-ribs sauce that is actually good for you!

Let's compare amounts per serving*:

- Traditional Bolognese: 472 calories, 19.7 grams of fat
- Vegan Bolognese: 158 calories, 7.8 grams of fat

Only two tablespoons of oil are added to a medley of fresh herbs, vegetables, and tempeh (optional). Allowing this ragu to simmer for 2 hours creates deeply complex and robust flavor.

For a gluten-free option, omit the tempeh and use wheat free pasta!

* According to recipe calculator.

Step 1: Ingredients

This is a very flexible recipe. I chose roasted eggplant and smoked tempeh to create a hearty, smoky center for the sauce. You could use fresh eggplant that has been sliced, salted, and allowed to drain. You could use smoked or baked tofu. You could use any sort of "meat substitute" you so desire, or just load up on veg.

- 1 onion, finely chopped
- 6 garlic cloves, finely chopped
- 2 celery ribs, finely chopped
- 1 medium carrot, finely chopped
- 2 tablespoons cup extra-virgin olive oil
- 1 package smoked tempeh or tofu (optional) chopped
- ½ cup dry red wine
- 1 pound eggplant, roasted or salted and drained, and chopped
- ¼ cup tomato paste
- ½ cup stewed tomatoes (can substitute for canned)
- ½ cup water
- ½ teaspoon fresh thyme
- Few shavings of fresh nutmeg (optional)

Step 2: Prep Ingredients

Chop up your ingredients so they're all ready to go in. Plan on an hour to prepare your eggplant, whether you roast it or not. I prefer the rich, smoky flavor of roasted eggplant. To achieve this, I split the eggplant in half, scored

mediterranean

down the middle of the flesh on each half, and roasted on an oiled baking sheet, flesh side down, for 20 minutes at 400°F.

Step 3: Sauté Veggies

Sauté the onion, garlic, carrot, and celery in oil in a heavy saucepan over medium heat, until softened—5 to 7 minutes.

Step 4: Add Tempeh

Add smoked tempeh and cook over medium high heat, stirring for about 6 minutes. If you've chosen not to roast your eggplant, add it along with the tempeh.

Step 5: Add Wine

Stir in wine and allow it to simmer until the liquid evaporates.

Step 6: Add Remaining Ingredients

Stir in eggplant (if you haven't yet), tomatoes, tomato paste, water, fresh thyme, and a shaving of nutmeg, and gently simmer, covered, until sauce is thickened (one to one and a half hours). Add salt and pepper and remove from heat.

mediterranean

Step 7: Add Pasta

Cook up your pasta to just before al dente. Stir it into the sauce and simmer to finish cooking. This is one of those dishes that's even better the second day! What's great is that you can make up a huge batch and freeze it for a month (without the added pasta).

Vegan Spinach Quiche with Brown Basmati Crust

By ShopCookMake
(http://www.instructables.com/
id/Vegan-Spinach-Quiche-with-
Brown-Basmati-Crust/)

When I became a vegan, I thought I had to say good bye to all my favorite foods. Quickly, I learned that was not the case. With a little imagination and creativity, I could enjoy all my favorite foods guilt free.

This is the most delicious quiche I've ever made in my life! It can be made a million different ways. It's also very healthy because it doesn't have any eggs or animal products—that means zero cholesterol and only good fats.

The texture is very creamy but firm, so it will hold its shape. You can definitely turn it into mini-quiches. This recipe serves four or five people, depending on how hungry they are.

Step 1: Ingredients

For the Quiche Filling

- 10 ounces extra-firm silken tofu
- 2 tablespoons soy milk
- 2 tablespoons nutritional yeast (optional)
- 2 teaspoons corn starch
- 1 teaspoon onion powder
- ⅛ teaspoon turmeric
- ⅛ teaspoon cumin
- Salt and pepper to taste

For the Vegetables:

- 1½ cups broccoli
- 3 cups fresh spinach (or ¾ cup frozen)
- 2 cloves garlic
- ¼ cup green pepper (or any color you like)
- ¼ cup onion
- ½ cup diced fresh tomato
    For the crust, you need ¾ cup brown basmati rice.

Step 2: Making the Crust

It's very simple to make this crust. Just cook the rice in 2½ cups of water for 45 minutes. The rice should be cooked over medium heat for the first 25 minutes and with the heat turned down to low and with a lid over the pot for the last 20 minutes. After the rice is done, it will have a firm texture and it'll be moist—that's what we're looking for. It'll be crispier after it comes out of the oven. If you didn't before, add some salt and pepper. You can also add 2 tablespoons of the filling to make the crust creamier instead of crunchy. Press the rice into the baking dish to form a crust. See the picture below.

21

Step 3: Making the Tofu Mix and Vegetables

In a blender, process all the ingredients for the quiche filling until smooth and put it in the fridge. Don't add too much turmeric because it'll give the dish a bitter taste. Then in a pan with a little oil, cook the vegetables together, except for the spinach. If you don't want to add extra fat, just cook with 3 tablespoons water, which is what I did. When all the veggies are cooked, add the spinach and mix well. After you have incorporated the quiche filling that was prepared earlier and the veggies in a bowl, pour it over the rice crust. Bake it for 35 to 45 minutes and let it rest for at least 15 minutes before cutting. It couldn't be easier.

Easy Pattypan Mini Souffle

By laxap
(http://www.instructables.com/
id/Easy-Pattypan-Mini-Souffle/)

Pattypan squash is a less-known cousin to pumpkins. It looks funny, can grow up to a moderate size, and tastes very delicate and slightly sweet when young and small.

Here is a soufflé recipe that is quite simple. In particular, it does not involve separating egg yolks from white and beating the latter.

Step 1: Gather Ingredients

For two small pattypans:
- 1 egg
- 100 grams cheese (Gruyere, Tilsit, Jura)
- 1 deciliter cream
- Pepper

You will also need some wax paper. This recipe is only about the pattypans, so you should additionally plan the other parts of your meal.

Step 2: Prep the Pattypans

Carefully cut off the top part. Hollow out the pattypan. Keep the top part for decoration, cutting it thinner if needed. Steam for approximately 2 minutes.

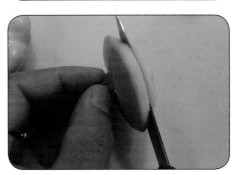

23

mediterranean

Step 3: Make the Filling

Mix one egg. Add grinded cheese, cream, and some pepper. Optionally, add some pressed garlic.

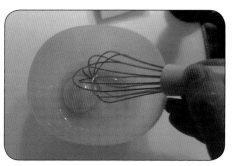

Step 4: Bake

Pre-heat oven: 360°F (180°C), middle to slightly low rack position. Cut a band of wax paper. Staple it to form a ring. It must fit into the hole. Carefully add the filling, not exceeding the top of the pattypan. Bake for approximtely 45 minutes. Meanwhile, cook any other things you have planned.

Constantly check your oven. The top of the soufflé must not burn. Due to the fact that the heat has to cross the pattypans, it takes a bit longer to bake than traditional small soufflés. If it is still liquid but brown on top, switch the heating to bottom only. When the filling is moderately firm (but not hard—must be similar to a soft flan), take out of oven and carefully remove the wax paper.

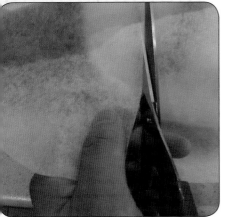

Step 5: Serve

Serve with rice or noodles and anything else you want. Add spices according to your liking. Bon appétit!

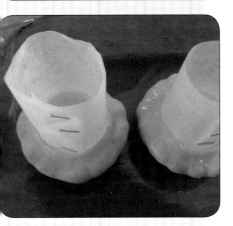

Vegetarian French Onion Soup

By shesparticular
(http://www.instructables.com/id/
Vegetarian-French-Onion-Soup/)

Sweet, caramelized onions in a rich stock covered in melted cheese—it doesn't get much better than that! French onion soup is awesome, but it's usually made with beef stock, which is problematic for vegetarians. With a few simple ingredients, it's easy to whip up some awesome French onion soup that will please any non-carnivore.

Note: As indicated below, vegan cheese can be substituted if desired (for the vegan folks), and the bread can be substituted with a gluten-free and gum-free bread or one with the parmesan cheese replaced with gruyere, and the flour can be omitted or replaced with corn starch dissolved in warm stock (for the gluten-free folks).

who avoid gluten, use gluten-free and gum-free bread or one with the parmesan cheese replaced with gruyere.)
- Approximately 4 ounces Gruyere cheese, shaved thin (more cheese can be added if desired; substitute vegan cheese if desired)
- 2 cups vegetable stock
- 1 tablespoon butter (or margarine or oil if making vegan)
- 1 tablespoon flour (omit or replace with a tablespoon of cornstarch dissolved in warm stock if making gluten-free)
- 1 teaspoon balsamic vinegar
- 1 clove garlic, finely minced
- 1 clove garlic, cut in half
- Salt (probably won't be needed unless you're a huge salt fan)
- Pepper
- Herbs to taste

Hardware
- Large skillet
- Very sharp knife
- Vegetable peeler
- Small sauce pot with fitted lid
- 2 oven-safe ramekins or other small soup crocks (each 10 ounces)

Step 1: You'll Need

Software

(Note: The following is for two servings; for more just multiply the amounts.)
- One large sweet onion, sliced very thin
- 2 or 3 slices French bread (day old, approximately ½ inch thick) (For folks

tep 2: Prepping and Cooking Onions

Cut both ends off of the onion and make a slit through one side from top to bottom so that you can remove the peel and outermost layer. Cut the onion in half, and slice each half into very thin slices. Melt butter in a large saucepan and add onions. Cook over low/medium heat stirring occasionally until the onions are translucent and beginning to brown. Transfer the onions to a small sauce pot, making sure to scrape the pan well. Add the stock, flour, vinegar, and garlic to the pot and stir well. Cover and cook over low heat for approximately 20 minutes until the stock has thickened slightly and the onions are very soft and tender. Add pepper and/or other herbs or spices as desired. (Keep in mind that you'll be adding salty cheese to the top, so you likely won't want to add salt to the stock and onions at this point since it's plenty salty as is.)

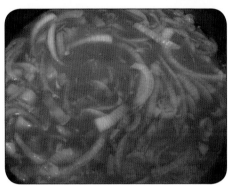

Step 3: Bread and Cheese

Cut several slices from a small loaf of day-old French bread—each approximately ½ inch thick. Lightly toast the bread slices and rub each with a cut clove of garlic. Using a vegetable peeler, shave thin pieces from a block of Gruyere cheese (can also be shredded if desired).

mediterranean

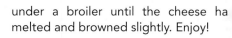

under a broiler until the cheese ha melted and browned slightly. Enjoy!

Step 4: Assembly

Fill each ramekin approximately ¾ inch from the top with stock and onions. Place a slice of bread into the ramekin and press down gently. If one slice doesn't fully cover the broth and onions you can add smaller pieces from another slice. Top with shaved or shredded Gruyere cheese. Place the ramekins

Spicy Chickpeas with Feta and Oregano

By garnishrecipes
(http://www.instructables.com/
id/Spicy-Chickpeas-with-Feta-
and-Oregano/)

In between grocery trips or before an extended trip, my cupboards have little more than dried beans and a few spices. At first glance, working with a limited ingredient base can be discouraging. However, cheese and herbs go a long way towards empty cupboard gourmet.

With a sprig of oregano from our patio herb garden, an extra nub of feta, and a sprinkle of intense cayenne, my limited supply of chickpeas became a simple yet satisfying dinner. I added a squeeze of lemon to the beans and cayenne for a little extra tartness. You can toss the beans in a tablespoon of apple cider vinegar for the same effect if your cupboard happens to be lean that day.

Step 1: Ingredients

This recipe serves four.
- 2 cups chickpeas, cooked
- 1 lemon, halved and seeded OR
  1 tablespoon apple cider vinegar
- 1 tablespoon olive oil
- 3 tablespoons feta, crumbled
- 1 tablespoon oregano, finely chopped
- ¼ teaspoon kosher salt
- ¼ teaspoon cayenne pepper
- Black pepper

Step 2

Boil the beans, if necessary. A quick method for beans (2 hours preparation time), is to bring the beans to a rolling boil for two minutes, let stand for an hour, and simmer for one hour. I like to add salt and a bay leaf to the beans a the 45-minute mark.

Step 3

When your beans are ready, toss them with one squeezed lemon, or a tablespoon of apple cider vinegar, and the tablespoon of olive oil. Add the cayenne and toss again.

Step 4

Divide into a serving bowl, or four individual side dishes, and spoon the crumbled feta evenly over each bowl.

Step 5

Finely chop the oregano leaves and distribute evenly as well.

Step 6

Add a pinch of sea or kosher salt, a twist of pepper, and serve.

Moroccan Stew (Vegan)

By SpamDam
(http://www.instructables.com/
id/Moroccan-Stew/)

This is a fresh and simple twist on Moroccan cooking with a base of tomatoes, lentils, and spices. In this vegetarian version, butternut squash fills the role of beef. It's a hearty, healthy, and spicy stew to provide warmth and energy in winter. While I've prepared this in a Crockpot, I've included instructions for those of you who don't have one. Moroccan stew makes a great stand-alone meal, and also works well on top of couscous or alongside hearty whole-grain bread.

Step 1: Ingredients and Equipment

Ingredients

For a 6-quart recipe, you'll need:

- 1 butternut squash
- 1 can stewed tomatoes
- 1 can chickpeas
- ⅔ cup split red lentils
- ⅓ cup chili flakes
- 1 cube vegetable bouillon
- 1 teaspoon cinnamon

Equipment

- Vegetable peeler
- Kitchen knife
- Cutting board
- Large metal spoon
- 6-quart Crockpot or large stewpot

Step 2: Prepare the Squash

Scrub the squash, then peel it with a vegetable peeler. Cut off the top and bottom ends. Chop off the base of the squash, then split the base down the middle to expose the core of seeds. Use a large metal spoon to scrape away the seeds and guts. Consider baking the seeds as a snack! Dice the squash into 1-inch cubes.

Step 3: Fill the Pot

Add the squash to the pot first, followed by stewed tomatoes, lentils, chickpeas, and spices. Pour in enough water to cover the ingredients. Stir well.

Step 4: Let It Simmer

Crockpot:

Cover the Crockpot and set to high heat for 4 hours, stir, and serve.

Stewpot:

Bring to a boil, stirring every five minutes. Reduce heat to a simmer and cook until the squash has a tender texture (try cutting it with a spoon).

mediterranean

Step 5: Enjoy!

Some of my favorite serving options are in a bowl alongside hearty bread or ladled over couscous. This stew makes great leftovers, as the flavor will mature the next day.

Homemade Spicy Eggplant Pizza

By skyisblu
(http://www.instructables.com/id/
Homemade-Spicy-Eggplant-Pizza/)

- ¼ cup grated parmesan
- 2 tablespoons olive oil
- 2 tablespoons minced garlic
- 2 fresh chilies, minced (I use red Thai chilies—if you prefer less heat, use less intense chilies like jalapeño)

As summer is nearing its transition into the cooler days of fall, it is the best time to make up something a little spicy using great seasonal vegetables and flavors. This is one of my favorite dishes to make on a cooler afternoon after a trip to the farmer's market or to my garden. This pizza really highlights the earthiness of the eggplant, and kicks it out of its natural blandness with a dose of garlic and chili oil. Enjoy!

Step 1: What You'll Need

For the Pizza Dough

- 1½ cups hot water (as hot as you can run it from the tap, not boiling or you will kill the yeast)
- 1½ teaspoons dry active yeast
- 1 tablespoon olive oil
- 1 tablespoon salt
- 1 tablespoon sugar
- 3 cups all-purpose flour
- Oil for greasing the bowl

For the Eggplant Topping

- 1 large eggplant
- Olive oil for brushing
- ¾ cup grated mozzarella

Step 2: Making the Pizza Dough

Note: This dough recipe is good for two pizzas, so if you want two eggplant pizzas, just double the amount of eggplant topping ingredients. Or you could top that second pizza with anything else you want.

This dough recipe is one that I have had since I was in grade-eight Home Economics class, and it has never failed. It makes great pizzas every time and can also be used for tasty calzones, or even an easy focaccia.

Sprinkle the yeast over the top of the hot water. Use the hottest water that you can run from your kitchen tap. Do not use boiling water or you will kill the yeast, and your dough will not rise. Let the yeast "bloom" for 5 minutes. Add the olive oil, sugar and salt to the yeast, and stir. Measure the flour into a large bowl. Add the yeast mixture to the flour and, using a wooden spoon, stir until well combined. The dough will appear very gooey—this is normal, as it makes a much more tender dough. Do not add more flour to the dough during this step.

Brush or spray some oil over the sides of the bowl and the top of the

35

dough. Flip the ball of dough over and oil the other side. This will help when removing the dough after rising. Cover the bowl with a clean kitchen towel, and set in a warm location to rise for an hour. Looking for a warm location? Try above the fridge, above your cabinets, or on the stove as you're preheating the oven for the next step!

Step 3: Preparing the Toppings

Onto the good stuff—this is where you can easily diverge from the recipe and top your pizza however you want, but I strongly suggest spicy eggplants. If, however, you choose to go your own way, skip ahead to the next step for directions for how to bake the pizza.

Slice up the eggplant into ⅓-inch slices and spread them onto an aluminum foil-lined baking pan brushed with oil. Brush the tops of the eggplant slices with oil also. Broil the eggplants until lightly browned, then turn them over and broil them the same way on the other side. Set them aside for now.

In a small frying pan, heat the 2 tablespoons of oil over medium high heat. Add the minced garlic and chilies, and swirl the pan for about a minute. You don't want to sauté them, just heat them and infuse the oil with all of that garlicky-chili flavor. Remove the pan from the heat and set aside for now. Mix the mozzarella and parmesan cheeses together in a bowl. Now you are ready to garnish your pizza!

Step 4: Topping and Baking Your Pizza

Preheat the oven to 500°F. Set one rack in the lowest position in your oven. If you have a pizza stone, place it on the rack before you preheat, so that it can heat to the same temperature as the oven. If you don't have a pizza stone, you can just as easily bake the pizza on a baking sheet. A pizza stone is a good investment, however, as it makes for a nice crisp outside and tender inside to your pizza crust. I highly recommend it.

Generously flour a section of counter or a silpat* mat. This is a really important step. The dough is very sticky, and this is when you will be adding in enough flour to make it workable, but not so much as to make it tough. So flour the counter well, and the rolling pin, and the top of the dough. Roll out half the pizza dough, for one pizza, to ¾-inch thick. You can make it round, square, or free form in shape—I haven't found that either one tastes better than the other, but I've always like the rustic look of the free-form pizza.

*A silpat mat is a silicone baking mat that can be laid over your counter before flouring. It will make transferring the dough to the pizza stone easier, and it will make cleaning up a cinch. If you don't have one but *are* baking on a pizza stone, transfer your dough to a floured, reverse baking sheet, so you can then

37

slide the dough onto the stone once it is topped.

Now for the toppings: First sprinkle about a quarter of the cheese mixture over the dough. This will help the rest of the toppings adhere to the crust once baked. Lay the eggplant slices over the crust, leaving a ¾-inch edge for holding, and overlap the slices where necessary. Top with the remaining cheese mixture. Finally, drizzle the garlic-chili oil, garlic and chili included, over the top of the cheese. Make sure to drizzle it lightly and evenly over the entire pizza, or you will end up with pockets of heat—unless, of course, that is what you are going for!

If you floured your surface really well, this part should will be easy. However, I have made this pizza half a dozen times, and this step has not gotten any easier. Using the help of a large spatula, slide the pizza off the counter and onto your baking sheet, or if you are using a stone, off the silpat or reversed baking sheet and onto the stone. Don't worry about squishing and smushing the pizza as you move it; you can adjust its size slightly once in the oven. Be careful not to burn yourself on the pizza stone—it is currently at 500°F! Close the oven and bake the pizza for 12 to 15 minutes, depending on how brown you like your crust, and how hot your oven runs. Remember: no two ovens are the same.

Bask in the awesomeness of a spicy, garlicky, cheesy eggplant plant pizza, with its tender, crisp homemade crust—oh yum. Grab your pizza wheel and slice into that bad boy and enjoy.

Remember, there's still enough dough left for a second pizza, so you could always recreate this one you could make something of your own creation.

Step 5: Yum!

Oooh, this is the best part. Once that timer rings, remove the pizza from the oven, either on its baking sheet or using a pair of tongs to slide it off the stone and onto a cutting board. Turn off the oven.

mediterranean

Creamy Vegan Mushroom Spinach Sauce

By resitton
(http://www.instructables.com/
id/Vegan-Creamy-Mushroom-
Spinach-Sauce/)

Craving a little creamy comfort sauce? Give this one a try. I served it over spaghetti squash, but you could use the pasta or rice of your choice. Feel free to add whatever vegetables you want. I added spinach; you could use kale or broccoli as well. I will throw in the step for cooking the spaghetti squash for those interested. It yields about four to five servings and takes about 15 minutes to prepare the sauce.

Ingredients

- 4 tablespoons of dairy-free soy margarine (I like Earth Balance.)
- 2 large cloves garlic, minced
- 16 ounces sliced mushrooms
- ½ to 1 cup of spinach (depends on how much you like; I use frozen when I don't have fresh)
- 1 tablespoon all-purpose flour (I use soy flour)
- 1 cup plain soy milk
- ¼ cup dairy-free sour cream
- ¼ teaspoon salt, plus more to taste
- Freshly ground black pepper, to taste

Step 1: Sauté Vegetables

In a large sauté pan, heat 2 tablespoons of the soy margarine over medium-high heat. Add the garlic, mushrooms, and spinach. Cook until the mushrooms are fragrant and soft, about 4 minutes. Transfer the mushrooms and garlic to a large bowl and set aside.

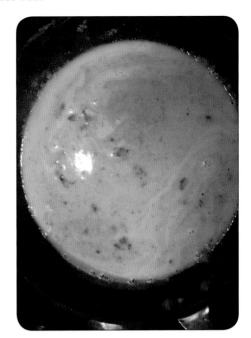

Step 2: Making the Cream Sauce

In the same sauté pan over medium-high heat, heat the remaining 2 tablespoons soy margarine and the flour, whisking constantly to combine and avoid burning, for about 45 seconds to 1 minute. Continuing to stir constantly, gradually add the soy milk until the mixture is smooth. Add the dairy-free sour cream, salt, and pepper, and stir until well combined. Add the mushrooms, spinach, and garlic to the sauce, and cook for about 2 minutes more.

Step 3: Serve

Remove the pan from heat. Add the pasta to the sauce and toss to coat the noodles. Portion the pasta, rice, spaghetti squash, etc. onto individual plates and add freshly ground pepper to taste. Serve immediately.

Step 4: Roasting a Spaghetti Squash

Roasting a spaghetti squash is very simple:
1. Preheat oven to 350°F.
2. Wash the squash.

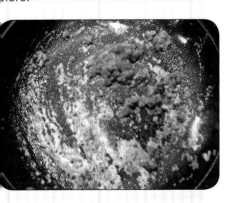

3. Cut the squash in half lengthwise.
4. Remove stringy seeds and pulp. Discard.
5. Rub olive or plant-based oil on both sides of the squash.
6. Sprinkle inside of squash halves with salt and pepper to taste.
7. Place cut side down onto a baking pan.
8. Place in preheated oven and roast for about 45 minutes.
9. Remove from oven.
10. Using fork, scoop out the inside of the squash (it will be stringy).
11. Season with salt and pepper and serve with sauce of your choice or as a side to another dish.

Very sweet and I love using i instead of pasta for most of my sauce: Spaghetti Squash is a lower calori alternative to pasta and rice. It is full c Vitamin A, folate, and calcium.

Italian Vegan Rice Patties

By LaVegetariana
(http://www.instructables.com/
id/Italian-Vegan-Rice-Patties/)

Serves about eight.

Step 1: Ingredients

2½ cups cooked rice
1 clove garlic, minced
Salt
Black pepper
Red pepper
Garlic powder
Parsley

- ½ cup soymilk
- 2 tablespoons vegan mayo
- 1 cup bread crumbs
- 1 cup shredded mozzarella (vegan or non-vegan)
- Canola oil for frying
- Bread crumbs for coating
- Marinara sauce for dipping
- Add onion, red pepper, green pepper for added flavor and color

Step 2: Directions

Mix all ingredients together in a mixing bowl. Set a large frying pan over medium heat with canola oil ready to fry the rice patties. Coat the patties in breadcrumbs and place in the hot oil to fry, crisp, and melt the cheese. Serve with marinara sauce and enjoy!

Raw Sundried Tomato Cashew Pesto Sauce and Zucchini Pasta

By naturesknockout
(http://www.instructables
.com/id/Raw-Sundried-Tomato-
Cashew-Pesto-Sauce-Zucchini-/)

This is gluten-free, dairy-free, and soy-free.

Step 1: Ingredients

- ¼ cup sundried tomatoes (fill water in cup and soak while setting up)
- 1 fresh tomato
- ½ cup raw cashews
- 1 handful fresh chives (or 1 scallion)
- 1–2 cloves fresh garlic
- ½–1 teaspoon dehydrated red chili peppers (depending on heat tolerance)
- 1 teaspoon sea salt
- ½ teaspoon dulce or kelp
- 1 teaspoon fresh peppercorns, ground
- 1 teaspoon dry oregano
- 1 teaspoon Italian Seasoning
- 2 tablespoons lime juice
- 2 tablespoons extra-virgin olive oil (cold pressed)
- 1–2 zucchinis (depending on size)

Step 2: Directions

Combine all ingredients (except zucchini and olive oil) in the blender. Let blend about 4 minutes to warm while preparing zucchini noodles. Use a spiral slicer for zucchini to get an angel hair pasta noodle. Place raw zucchini in slicer and prepare noodles. Add olive oil to the pesto sauce and pulse once or twice. Stir sauce into noodles and serve. Makes two to four servings.

This recipe is brought to you by Laurie of naturesknockout.com.

Risotto with Porcini, Red Wine, and Sage

By nonreactivepan
(http://www.instructables.com/
id/Risotto-with-Porcini-Red-
Wine-and-Sage/)

If you're not from San Francisco, d like you to know that we don't get ummer weather until the last week in eptember or in early October. It is always n odd time of year for me because the ght is changing and I expect a chill in the ir, just like when I was little in New York.

This time of year (no matter what 1e weather) always makes me want o have warm, satisfying rice or pasta ishes. The other day I decided to break ut my stand-by risotto recipe. It's fairly imple and oh-so-satisfying.

Just a note: the only dairy product 1 this recipe is butter: I can't seem to emove it completely from my repertoire. here's just no replacement for the flavor nd creaminess butter brings to rice. ut, if you'd like to make this completely egan, replace the butter with olive oil.

1gredients

4 bouillon cubes (I use porcini cubes)
4 cups water
1 bag dried porcini mushrooms
1 cup red wine (or enough to fully cover the dried porcini mushrooms)
3 tablespoons butter
2 tablespoons olive oil
3 cloves garlic, minced
2 cups Arborio rice
4 fresh sage leaves, minced (or ¼ teaspoon dried sage)
Salt, pepper, and red pepper to taste

Step 1: Getting Started

Make the Stock

Heat the bouillon and the water in a large saucepan. Bring to a boil, making sure all the cubes dissolve completely. Lower to a simmer and stir occasionally until it is time to add the liquid to the rice.

I love porcini mushrooms. When I discovered this bouillon, I just about fell over in glee. It is amazing how strongly the mushroom flavors come through. In general, I'm more of a chicken stock kind of girl, and I do not care for veggie stock. It usually tastes way too much like celery for my liking. But these cubes make it possible to have the best of a non-meat based bouillon and a well flavored broth all in one.

Soak the Dried Porcini

Pour the cup of red wine into a small saucepan. Add the porcini mushrooms, making sure there is enough wine to completely submerge them. Bring the

45

wine to a boil, then reduce to a simmer. Keep simmering for about 15 minutes, until the mushrooms are soft. Pour the wine and mushrooms through a sieve or strainer, making sure to capture all of the liquid in a bowl beneath the strainer. Chop mushrooms coarsely and set aside.

Start the Rice

Again, porcini is my favorite. Any chance I have to add them to a dish, I take it. The dried ones are usually what I have on hand, and they work well. In San Francisco, there is a whole mushroom booth at the giant Ferry Building farmer's market. We're lucky enough to get frozen fresh porcini there. It costs an arm and a leg, but the flavor is so intense you don't need to use that much, so a bag lasted me for a good six months in the freezer. The red wine makes the depth of the earthy flavors shine through. If you can afford to use a higher quality cup of wine here, you'll taste the difference.

Step 2: Arborio

Heat a large, heavy-bottomed pot over medium heat. Add butter and allow to melt, then add the olive oil. Lower heat to medium-low and add the minced garlic. Sauté garlic until almost opaque. Add rice, stirring to cover all the grains in the butter/oil mixture.

Quite simply, you are trying to get the rice to cook slowly so that it will toast somewhat in the beginning and then take

its time absorbing all of the lovely stock and wine you are going to add to it.

Take your time here, and if it seems things are starting to stick or burn, lower the heat and relax. If you like a glass of wine, now's a good time to grab one before you get ready to stir for a bit.

Step 3: Cook That Rice

Add ½ cup of stock to the rice pot, stirring constantly. As soon as the stock has been completely absorbed, add another ½ cup and stir until absorbed. Alternating ½ cup of stock and ½ cup of wine, continue adding liquid and stirring to absorb until all the liquid has been added. The rice should be soft and ready to eat once all the liquid has been incorporated. Remove the pot from the heat and add the sage, salt, pepper, and red pepper flakes to the rice. This is the most time consuming step, but again, just take it slow—and don't worry, you'll be eating soon enough.

Make sure that all of the liquid gets absorbed before you make a move to add more. It's tough to wait, I know; I've rushed it before and regretted it after the fact. The rice needs time to soak it all up before it takes another breath and is ready to drink up some more. It'll be well worth your effort (and the number of pans you'll have to clean). It's a great fall dish, especially if you live somewhere where the weather has actually started to shift to coolness.

Section 2
Middle Eastern

Easy Savory Winter Vegetable Stew with Quinoa

By tesseliot
(http://www.instructables
.com/id/Easy-Savory-Winter-
Vegetable-Stew-with-Quinoa/)

This is a really tasty vegetable stew that, thanks to quinoa, has a complete protein but no gluten or cholesterol. You can live off this for days and not need any other protein. I am a big pepper fan, so you can adjust downward if you don't like that taste.

It's very simple to make and throw into the crock pot to cook overnight. It is especially good to know it's a healthy meal, low in calories. If you are gluten intolerant, rice crisps add a nice crunch as a side dish.

I can't say enough good things about the quinoa. It can be made as a side dish, with broth instead of water, and mixed with stir fry. This in particular is my favorite veggie mix.

Tip: Chopping or dicing the veggies is important—your spoon should pick up lots of different tastes, as opposed to one big mouthful of potato or turnip. Mixing those finely chopped ingredients means a different mix with every spoonful, and makes this so nice to eat. It's not boring mouthful to mouthful. Lots of us forget the more old-fashioned turnip or rutabaga, both of which are nutritious and tasty in soup. For any of you with sugar issues, use less potato or none at all. It will still taste good.

Step 1: Ingredients and Equipment

- A gallon-sized crock pot
- 2 boxes organic vegetable broth
- 2 onions, diced (a chopped up leek is mixed in, too)
- 2 boxes of crushed or chopped tomatoes
- 2 potatoes, chopped into ½-inch cubes
- 2 carrots, diced
- 1 large turnip, chopped into ½-inch cubes
- About ½ cup of diced rutabaga
- Fresh dill, about 3 tablespoons chopped up
- Fresh parsley, about 4 tablespoons chopped up
- A few stalks of celery, chopped finely (I pulled off three, but ate one with some peanut butter)
- 1 tablespoon black pepper
- 1 teaspoon paprika
- 1 tablespoon Worcestershire sauce (vegans can skip this)
- Garlic, 3 cloves minced, or 1 teaspoon powdered
- Salt
- 1 cup pre-washed red quinoa (put in last)
- Garnishes: grated cheddar or sour cream

Step 3: Add the Quinoa

The next morning, put in the cup of quinoa and keep the pot on high for at least a half hour. You can turn it down to low when the quinoa is cooked—it only takes about 20 minutes or so (I like to give it an hour at lower crock-pot temperatures). It will really thicken the soup. Inca red quinoa just disappears in a tomato base dish but adds a lovely flavor without the cholesterol in meat. It is ready to eat at any point after that. I am still finishing this batch two days later, still delicious and still not spoiled because there is no fat to go rancid. If you get bored eating it for days, feed your hungry friends or freeze it in individual servings.

Step 2: My Favorite Step

Throw everything in the pot before you go to bed and cook overnight on high. Have wonderful dreams of your soon-to-be delicious soup for lunch or dinner the next day. Feel great that your body is not going to be awash in fat. All that chopping worked up an appetite, right? You can see in the picture that I like to be amused while chopping. I do keep a careful eye on where my knife is relative to my fingers, no matter how funny the entertainment is, or how hot the toddy.

Quinoa Burgers

By leah_e
(http://www.instructables.com/
id/Quinoa-Burgers/)

Suitable for gluten free, lactose free, low FODMAP diet (makes eight to ten).

Step 1: Ingredients

- 150 grams quinoa, prepared according to packet
- 1 courgette, grated
- 2 eggs (beaten)
- 100 grams crumbled feta
- Bunch of coriander, chopped
- 50 grams pumpkin seeds
- 50 grams sunflower seeds
- 1 teaspoon cumin seeds
- ½ teaspoon tamari (or soy sauce if you are okay with gluten)
- 50 grams oats
- 50 grams spelt flour
- Juice of ½ lemon
- 3–4 tablespoons oil for shallow frying

Step 2: Directions

1. Begin by draining or squeezing liquid out of the courgette. Do this either in your hands, or place courgette in a seive, with a bowl on top weighted down with a can for 30 minutes.
2. In a heavy-based pan, toast the seeds on a low heat for 5 to 10 minutes. Turn off the heat if they begin to pop. Transfer to a bowl and pour ½ teaspoon soy sauce onto warm seeds. Stir to mix.
3. In a large bowl, mix quinoa, coriander, courgette, 2 eggs, and lemon juice. Add the seeds and the crumbled feta.
4. Now add the oats and flour a little at a time. You may need more or less than the amount stated depending on how liquid-y your mixture is. Keep adding until you can form the mix into a ball that will hold its shape.
5. Form the mixture into round patties; each one should have around 2 tablespoons of the mixture. Meanwhile, heat the oil (I used olive oil) in a large pan.
6. When the oil is hot, put four to five patties into the pan to cook over a low-medium heat. After 5 minutes, when it is golden brown on one side, flip over and cook on the other side.
7. Remove patties from the pan onto a piece of kitchen roll to remove excess oil.

Chickpea and Carrot Tangine

By jessyratfink
(http://www.instructables.com/
id/Chickpea-and-carrot-tangine/)

A quick and easy vegan meal for nights when you want something fast. It's also something I make when I get to the end of my groceries as I always have these ingredients on hand.

Step 1: Ingredients

- 1 small onion, diced (or half a large one)
- 1 14½-ounce can chickpeas, drained
- 2 carrots, cut into slices
- 2–3 cloves garlic, minced
- ½ teaspoon cumin
- ½ teaspoon turmeric
- Good pinch cinnamon
- Good pinch cayenne
- Salt and pepper to taste
- 1 cup water
- 1 cup rice (anything you like)
- 1¾ cup water
- Salt

Step 2: Cook the Veggies

Put a little olive oil in your pan over medium heat and dump in the veggies. Let them cook for a few minutes or until the onions get translucent and the carrots begin to soften.

Step 3: Add the Spices, Chickpeas, and Garlic

Stir it together very well and let it cook for a couple minutes. You want the spices and garlic to get really fragrant—then you'll know you're ready!

Step 4: Add Water and Simmer

Add the water and mix, and let it come up to a boil. Then turn it down to a simmer and cover it. You'll let this cook for about 20 minutes covered.

Step 5: Make the Rice

While it simmers, you'll have just enough time to make some rice. I always do 1 cup of rice and 1¾ cup of water. Bring the cup of water to a boil with a generous pinch of salt, pour in the rice, and turn the heat to low and cover. Cook for 18 minutes; turn off the heat, let sit covered for an additional 10 minutes, and then fluff with a fork. I don't use any butter or oil, but feel free to add some if you'd like.

Step 6: Check the Liquid Level and Serve

After 20 minutes, the liquid should have reduced quite a bit. If not, turn up the heat and let it simmer uncovered for a few minutes while your rice finishes up getting nice and fluffy. You still want it to be slightly runny (the liquid is excellent once it soaks into the rice) but not a soup. This is also a good time to check the seasonings and add more as desired. Spoon it over rice and eat! Cilantro and parsley are good with this, as is sriracha.

middle eastern

Baked Falafel Recipe

By jessyratfink
(http://www.instructables.com/
id/Baked-Falafel-Recipe/)

I love falafel. So very much. But I really
ate frying things. The smell of oil, the
ness, the flesh wounds. Just not a good
ituation. And the flesh wounds might not
et you enjoy your yummy falafel. Baked
alafel is obviously the answer.

Step 1: Ingredients and Equipment

- 15–20-ounce can chickpeas, drained OR 1 cup dried chickpeas, soaked for 24 hours and drained
- ½ onion
- 6 tablespoons of chopped parsley and/or cilantro (I'm doing about two-thirds parsley, one-third cilantro)
- 2–3 cloves garlic, depending on your taste
- 1 teaspoon cumin
- 2 teaspoons coriander
- 1 teaspoon chili powder
- Pinch of cayenne
- Couple tablespoons of olive oil (for the falafel and for the baking sheet)
- Salt and pepper to taste
- A food processor

It is important to note that I am using cooked chickpeas, which is fine. But if you'd like to get all traditional, simply soak a cup of dried chickpeas in the fridge for 24 hours and use those. I'll be doing that next time to see the difference.

The falafel will be baked at 400°F—10 minutes for first side, 15 minutes for the second.

middle eastern

Step 2: Preheat and Prep

Turn the oven on to 400°F. Roughly chop the herbs, onions, and garlic. I know most people wonder why, but my food processor hates big pieces. I bet yours does too. So be nice to it.

Step 3: Process!

Throw everything in the food processor. You'll want to pulse it, scraping down the sides until everything is finely processed and combined, but not pureed. If you're having problems getting it to come together, add a tiny bit of olive oil to get it going. The mixture should be slightly wet and hold together well. Taste everything at this point and adjust seasonings as needed.

Step 4: Oil the Baking Sheet and Form Patties

I got ten patties out of the mixture. I started with balls about two inche wide and then flattened them. I lik having them flat because they're easie to eat in a pita and they cook better i the oven. You can do bigger or smalle but you might want to adjust th cooking time. Just play around with it.

Step 5: Cooking

After ten minutes, take them out and carefully flip them. They'll be starting to brown and should be pretty firm. Put them back in for 15 minutes. Once I took them out, I flipped them so you guys can see how lovely and brown they get. The outsides should be crusty, and the insides should be nice and soft.

Step 6: Serve!

Great with yogurt or sour cream, hummus, tahini sauce, guacamole, or tzatziki. I always put cucumber and red onion in mine. A little mint and tomato is good, too.

Tasty Lentils and Quinoa—a One Dish Meal

By berserk
(http://www.instructables.com/
id/Tasty-Lentils-and-Quinoa—a-
one-dish-meal/)

I could go on and on about the nutritional benefits of lentils (2 percent protein) and quinoa (one of the most balanced sets of essential amino acids in a vegetable, and still 12 percent to 18 percent). I think it's more important, though, that this is tasty enough to become one of our family favorites!

Step 1: Ingredients

In spite of its nutritional value, quinoa is not always easy to find. We usually get ours at Scoop-and-Weigh, the local bulk seller. If they have different kinds of quinoa, we usually get the red stuff, just because it adds a bit more color—they taste pretty similar to me. Your bulk seller usually also has a better deal on spices than your supermarket, but all other ingredients should be available at your supermarket.

Ingredients
- 1 tablespoon olive oil
- 2 onions, chopped
- 3 cloves garlic, minced
- 1.5 teaspoon ground cumin
- 1 teaspoon curry paste
- 0.5 teaspoon each cinnamon and salt
- 4 carrots, sliced
- 1 cup quinoa (pronounced kee nwa) or rice
- 2 cups vegetable stock
- 1 can (19 oz) lentils, drained and rinsed
- 1 apple, unpeeled and diced
- 4 green onions, sliced
- 0.5 cup plain yogurt

Step 2: How to Put It Together

Heat oil in a skillet or pan over medium heat. Cook onions, garlic, cumin, curry paste, cinnamon, and salt, stirring often for about 5 minutes or until softened. Stir in carrots and quinoa. Cook, stirring occasionally, for about 1 minute. Pour in stock and bring to a boil. Reduce heat, cover, and simmer for about 20 minutes until quinoa is tender and most of the liquid is absorbed. Stir in lentils, apple, and green onions. Cook for about 5 minutes or until lentils are heated through. Serve with a dollop of yogurt. I like a large dollop of yoghurt, because it adds a bit of a tang. Enjoy!

60

Section 3
Asian

Chana masala is one of my favorite Indian dishes to eat. Back when I lived in Louisville, I went to the same Indian buffet all the time with my friends. I went so often than the servers there began to recognize me. If chana masala was missing from the buffet during lunch, they would bring me out some of the chana masala they were making for dinner service. I think I could have eaten there every day if I had enough money!

I've been experimenting with making my own chana masala at home and I think I've finally got it right! It's spicy, sour, and sweet and has tons of depth.

Step 1: Ingredients

- 2 cans chickpeas, drained and rinsed OR 4 cups chickpeas, drained and rinsed (I really like cooking my own chickpeas if I have time!)
- ¾ cup water
- 1 14½-ounce can whole tomatoes
- 1 medium onion
- 1 Serrano pepper
- 2 cloves garlic
- 2 inches fresh ginger
- ¼ teaspoon Cayenne
- 2 teaspoons cumin
- 2 teaspoons coriander
- 1 teaspoon paprika
- 1 teaspoon turmeric
- 2 teaspoons garam masala
- 1 tablespoon amchur powder (also spelled amchoor)
- Fresh cilantro

This ingredients list might look crazy, but it's mostly spices. Many of them should be things you have on hand! The two ingredients I'm very picky about are the amchur powder and the garam masala. Make sure you have good quality garam masala—it should be slightly sweet and very fragrant. The amchur powder can be a little tricky to find, but most Indian groceries will have it, and I'm sure you can buy it online. Amchur powder is sour and fruity, made from green mangoes.

Step 2: Cut Up the Veggies and Measure out the Spices

Mince the onion, garlic, and Serrano pepper. (You can deseed the pepper if it seems too hot.) Roughly chop the tomatoes and set them aside—you'll add them later. Reserve the liquid in the can. Peel and grate the ginger (you'll want a couple teaspoons of ginger). At this point it's also awesome to measure out all the spices into a small bowl; it'll make everything quicker.

Step 3: Cook the Veggies and Add Spices

Add a couple tablespoons of neutral oil to a pan and heat over medium-high heat. Heat the oil until it shimmers, and then add the ginger, garlic, onion, and Serrano. Cook this for a few minutes, stirring often, until the onions begin to brown. Make sure to keep stirring so it doesn't burn! Once the onions begin to brown, add the spices and stir everything around for a couple minutes until everything smells yummy.

asian

Step 4: Add the Tomatoes, Chickpeas, and Water

Once the spices and veggies have cooked for a minute, add in the chopped tomatoes and stir well. Add in the reserved tomato juices from the can. Now pour in the chickpeas and the water and stir.

Step 5: Simmer!

Simmer with the lid on for at least 20 minutes. The longer, the better. The chickpeas take a little while to get all flavored up. If the liquid gets low, add more, ¼ cup at a time. I like my chana masala a little less saucy, so I let most of my liquid evaporate. Use this time to clean up the kitchen you just destroyed, or maybe make some rice. This is good with rice.

asian

65

because you never know how salty the chickpeas or tomatoes will be. Once it's properly salted, add some cilantro if you're into that and eat.

Step 6: Check Seasoning and Add Cilantro

I normally check for salt at this point. It will probably need a little. You just don't want to go crazy with it before

asian

Fiery Pumpkin Samosas

By wizgirl
(http://www.instructables.com/
id/Fiery-Pumpkin-Samosas/)

These fiery pumpkin samosas are *oh-so-delicioso*. Serve them with a spicy fruit chutney and some quality plain yogurt. This is a great way to use leftover pumpkin from your fresh pumpkin pie.

Filling

- 2½ cups pumpkin, cut into ½ inch cubes
- 1 large onion, diced
- 3 green chilies chopped
- 3 tablespoons raisins, soaked in warm water
- ¼ cup cilantro
- 1 teaspoon coriander powder
- 1 teaspoon ground cumin
- ½ teaspoon amchor powder (dry mango powder)
- 1 teaspoon ground ginger
- pinch asafoetida (aka stink finger)

Amchor powder and asafoetida can be found at your local Indian market.

asian

Step 1: Ingredients

- Samosa
- 2 cups flour
- 2 teaspoons oil
- Water

Step 2: The Dough

Mix the flour and oil. Add water and knead until you have a stiff dough. This dough does not require a lot of kneading. Dough should not be sticky; some cracks will still form. Let dough sit for 15 minutes.

Step 3: The Great Pumpkin

Mix the dry spices together. Heat a tablespoon of oil in a large pan in medium-high heat. Add the spices and heat until fragrant. Add all of the vegetables and stir to coat with oil and spices. Do not add the raisins and cilantro, these are added later. Sauté until onions begin to brown. Reduce heat. Add 2 tablespoons of water, cover, and cook until pumpkin is tender. Add raisins and cilantro and stir. Remove from heat, allow to cool slightly.

Step 4: Fill and Fry
Fill

Divide the dough into four balls. Roll a dough ball into an oval. Cut the oval in half. Wet the edges of the half oval, this will help seal the samosa. Fold the flat cut edge of the oval together forming a cone (see photos). Fill the cone with the vegetable mixture. Fold the rounded top over the cone and seal. Set the completed cone on a floured surface.

Fry

Heat the oil to 350°F. Fry samosas until they are golden brown. Carefully remove, and place samosas on a paper towel-lined plate to absorb excess oil.

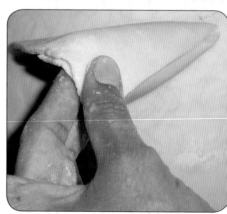

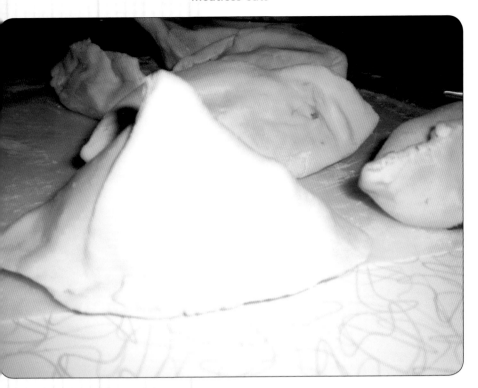

asian

How to Change the Texture of Tofu

By weekofmenus
(http://www.instructables.com/
id/How-to-change-the-texture-
of-tofu/)

Many people don't find the texture of tofu appealing, complaining of its watered-down texture, slimy texture, mushy texture, etc. But you can change the texture of tofu, and dramatically change your eating experience of it, to create really delicious stir fries like this one, after you've changed the texture.

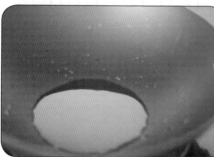

Step 1: Draining the Excess Water from Tofu

First cut your *firm* or *extra firm* tofu (not medium firm or silken tofu) into 1-inch cubes. Line a plate with two paper towels and allow excess water from tofu to drain into the paper towel. This step is very important, eliminating as much water as possible. Allow tofu to drain for 10 to 15 minutes. Your paper towels will be saturated.

Step 2: Preparing to Fry Tofu

Heat a wok over high heat and add vegetable oil.

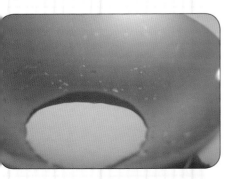

Step 3: Add Tofu to Oil

Add drained tofu, being careful as the oil can splatter.

Step 4: Fry until Golden

Fry, turning occasionally until tofu begins to turn golden brown. You have now changed the texture of your tofu. Enjoy this new texture in stir fries or just as it is.

asian

How to Cook Chinese Steamed Egg Soup

By yuhuaabc

(http://www.instructables
.com/id/How-to-cook-Chinese-
steamed-egg-soup/)

I'm going to teach you a very easy recipe—Chinese steamed egg soup! Steamed egg soup is a traditional dish of China, especially in the north. It's very easy and convenient, and it's also very delicious and nutritious! I always cook this dish for myself, and I never tire of it. You can also put some other vegetables in as you like, such as carrots, celery, etc.

Step 1: Ingredients and Equipment

Ingredients

- 2 eggs
- Leeks or chives
- Salt
- Chicken extract
- Pepper
- Cooking oil
- Sesame oil
- Parsley, celery, or carrots as you like

Equipment

- Food steamer
- A big bowl (15 centimeters)

Step 2: Process Ingredients

First, let's clean the vegetables and chop the leek and parsley. If you like celery (or carrots), you can also chop them. It's optional. But leeks or chives are necessary. Then crack the eggs into a bowl and beat the eggs until they are mixed well.

72

Step 3: Add Water and Spices

Add chopped leek (chopped celery, chopped carrots) into the egg and mix it. (Remember to first mix the egg and leek well.) Prepare warm boiled water, pour into the bowl in a ratio of nearly 1½:1 (water: egg). Then add salt (amount shown in the picture), some pepper, chicken, a little cooking oil, and sesame oil. If you like spicy, you can also put some chili oil. You can also add any spices you are partial to. Then mix them up.

Tips: You must use warm water, because if the water is cold, the egg and water can't mix well. You also don't want it to be scalding, as that will change the texture of the soup.

Step 4: Steam for Ten Minutes

Now that everything is prepared, we just need to cook it. Put the bowl into the food steamer, cover a plate onto the bowl, or use plastic wrap to cover, and poke some holes on it. In this way we can prevent vapor returning to the surface of the egg, causing the surface to become bumpy. Don't forget to put some water in the bottom of the steamer! When the water boils, put the bowl inside, reduce the heat, and steam for about ten minutes. Don't steam it for too long, or it will dry out and it won't be tasty. When the egg mixture has just become solid, then it's just right.

asian

73

Step 5: Done! Just eat!

Turn off the heat, and take the bowl out. Look how tender and smooth it is! At last, put the parsley inside it.

Potato and Cauliflower Curry

By jessyratfink
(http://www.instructables.com/
id/Potato-and-cauliflower-curry/)

This curry is a super easy and delicious meal if you have a well-stocked spice cabinet! The main ingredients in this curry are cauliflower and potatoes, but you can easily add some meat or additional veggies if you'd like!

I suppose this recipe is more of a course in wingin' it instead of set rules. I normally make up this recipe as I go along, but I tried to measure things out for once. And best of all, you can be eating in an hour!

Step 1: Ingredients

- 1 small cauliflower
- 1 onion
- 2–4 potatoes (you want the amount of potatoes to be equal to the amount of cauliflower)
- 2 small tomatoes
- 3–4 cloves garlic
- A handful of cilantro
- About 2 inches of ginger
- 1 tablespoon curry powder of choice
- ½ teaspoon cumin
- ½ teaspoon cumin seeds
- ½ teaspoon turmeric
- ½ teaspoon coriander
- ½ teaspoon chili powder
- Salt to taste
- ½ cup water or veggie/chicken stock if you're feeling fancy
- Jalapeño or other spicy pepper if you like

The cumin seeds are entirely optional, but I think it gives it a great taste. Love biting into one! I prefer red potatoes with the skin on for this recipe. And of course, feel free to leave the cilantro out if you hate it. Also, note that the spices are just good base amounts for the recipe—you can add even more if you like! More cumin seeds and chili powder always make a good curry. You're also going to need a big pot to cook this in. The flatter it can all get, the better it will cook.

Step 2: Prep the Veggies

Remove the stem from the cauliflower and chop it into smaller pieces, chop up the potatoes, and dice the onions and tomatoes. Mince the garlic and ginger and chop the jalapeño or other pepper as finely as you like if you're using it. Get a large pan with about a tablespoon of oil in it heating up over medium heat.

Step 3: Sautéing

Once the oil is hot, dump in the onions and hot pepper and cook them until softened. Then add in the garlic and ginger and cook until fragrant. At this point, add all of your spices along with a good pinch of salt. Stir this around until everything is nice and coated.

Step 4: Simmering!

Add the potatoes, cauliflower, and tomato to the pot and stir everything together. You want everything to get pretty orange at this point. Once everything is coated in oil and spices, add 1½ cups water or stock and stir again. (Note that if you added meat or additional veggies, you will need more liquid! I like the liquid level to be about ½ inch below the veggies) Now cover the pan, drop it down to a simmer, and let cook for 15 minutes.

asian

Once the 15 minutes are up, check for seasonings! I'll normally add a little more curry powder at this point, maybe a little more salt. It is good to ease into both things. If it's not spicy enough, add more chili powder or cayenne. If you'd like a little more acid, put in extra coriander—it's very citrusy and nice. Taste too sweet for you? Add a little turmeric.

Once everything tastes right to you, cover the pot and simmer for an additional 15 minutes minimum! If you have longer to simmer it, it'll be thicker and taste a little stronger. It's up to you.

Step 5: Serve!

Once it's cooked long enough for you, take it off the heat and chop up about a handful of cilantro and mix that in. It's super yummy with pickled red onions or spicy onion chutney or relish. Anything with a little vinegar or acid is a great friend of this curry, even hot sauces! Also good with naan or over a bowl of rice. Or just by itself! And any leftovers you have will taste even better.

asian

Miso Tofu Sandwiches

By nagutron
(http://www.instructables.com/
id/Miso-Tofu-Sandwiches/)

Delicious veggie sandwiches!

Step 1: Ingredients
- Tofu
- Miso soup mix
- Any other veggies of your choice

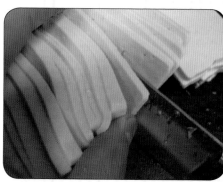

Directions

Dip the tofu in miso soup mix and then pan fry it. Add whatever other veggies you like. This time, I used onions, bell peppers, lettuce, tomatoes, and sprouts. Another delicious variant is to wrap the tofu slices in a strip of nori and fry that. It's crispy and great in sandwiches.

asian

Vegetarian Pho

By wizgirl
(http://www.instructables.com/
id/Vegetarian-Pho/)

When our favorite Pho restaurant was shut down because a Lowe's was moving in, I couldn't find a vegetarian version of the soup anywhere. This is a combination of recipes I found online. It's pho-king delicious!

Definition of Pho from Wikipedia: "Pho (Vietnamese pronunciation: [fuh]) is a Vietnamese noodle soup, usually served with beef (pho bo) or chicken (pho ga). [1] The soup includes noodles made from rice and is often served with basil, lime, bean sprouts, and peppers that are added to the soup by the consumer."

This recipe takes less than an hour and will make four large bowls of pho.

Step 1: Ingredients
Broth
- 60 ounces vegetarian broth
- 8 star anise
- 1–2 sticks cinnamon
- 8 cloves
- 1 thumb-sized piece of ginger, sliced
- 8 cloves of garlic, quartered
- 1–2 tablespoons soy sauce
- 2 onions, quartered
- 3 shallots, halved
- 6 cups water

Veggies (just some suggestions)
- Carrots
- Bok choy
- Broccoli
- Cauliflower

Noodles
- 1 package thin rice noodles

Pho Fixin's
- Fried tofu
- Jalapeño
- Lime
- Bean sprouts
- Cilantro
- Basil
- Mint
- Sriracha hot chili sauce

Step 2: Make the Broth
Heat a large pot over medium-high heat. Add the garlic, onions, star anise, cloves, and ginger to the pot. Stir over heat until it begins to brown. Add the broth, water, and soy sauce. Bring to a boil. Reduce heat and simmer for 30 minutes. Strain the broth into a new pot and reheat.

Step 3: Prepare the Fixin's

Wash the cilantro, basil, bean sprouts, and mint. Slice the jalapeño. Quarter the lime. Arrange everything on a plate.

Step 4: Prepare the Noodles

Prepare the noodles as described on the package. The one I used were immersed in boiling water for 10 to 15 seconds and then rinsed.

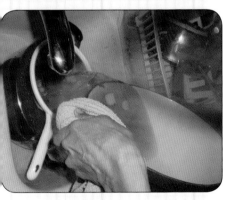

Step 5: Finish It

Add about a cup of noodles to the bottom of each bowl. Pour hot broth over the noodles. Add vegetables (carrots, broccoli, etc) and allow to sit for a few minutes. Add tofu. Serve with chopsticks, a spoon, Sriacha hot chili sauce, and the plate of fixin's. Everyone should add the fixin's to their soup as desired. Remove the jalapeños when it starts getting too spicy.

asian

Tom Kha Gai— Thai Coconut Soup

By canida
(http://www.instructables.com/
id/Tom-Kha-Gai-Thai-Coconut-
Soup/)

A traditional and tasty Thai soup, this is my favorite comparison point between Thai restaurants and an excellent twist on chicken soup for cold winter days. I'm a huge fan of coconut, chicken soup, and creamy soups in general, so it's a winner for me. Of course, making it at home means I can customize it to my preferences. It's surprisingly easy to make! This recipe is loosely adapted from David Johnson's Thai Food, a brick-sized comprehensive guide to Thai cooking. This is a vegetarian recipe. However, you could always use chicken stock or fish stock, fish sauce instead of soy sauce, and any meats you want in the dish if you're feeling carnivorous.

Step 1: Tools and Ingredients

This recipe scales beautifully—just multiply the ingredients below. I've included substitutions for ingredients you may not have easily at hand, but a trip to an Asian grocery will turn up everything on this list handily. I buy lots of lemongrass and galanga ahead, then chop and freeze it in pre-sorted zip-lock bags for future use. They keep quite well. You can also do this with the shallots, coriander root, and kaffir lime leaves.

Broth

- 1 can coconut milk
- 2–3 cups veg stock (homemade is best than the stuff in cartons; boullion cubes are a last resort)
- Pinch of salt
- 1 teaspoon palm sugar (I usually substitute brown sugar)
- 2 stalks fresh lemongrass, washed and chopped in chunks (Dried lemongrass is far inferior—punch it up with extra lime juice and zest at the end if you're forced to go this route.)
- 3 red shallots, peeled and chunked (I often substitute 3 smashed cloves of garlic plus a bit of onion)
- 2 coriander roots, scraped (I usually substitute a pinch of whole coriander seed plus a handful of fresh coriander [cilantro] leaves)
- 2 chili peppers, halved (pick your favorite type, and modify number to suit your spice taste)
- 1½-inch chunk of galanga root, chunked (Ginger is in the same family, but tastes totally different— galanga *totally* makes the flavor of this dish. If you can't get this locally, travel to a nearby city and visit the Asian markets or scour the Internet, buy a pound, then freeze what you can't use now. It's a floral flavor that you'll definitely recognize if you've had tom kha gai before.)
- 3 kaffir lime leaves, coarsely chopped (I have a kaffir lime tree in my yard, but you can substitute lime zest if necessary. It just won't be as fragrant and complex.)
- 1 teaspoon chili-garlic sauce (optional, and kind of a cheat, but often good)

asian

Chunks

- 1 pound tofu, cut to 1" pieces (or you can just use veggies if you want)
- 1 cup chopped mushrooms (your choice—mix it up)
- 1–3 soy sauce
- 1 can baby corn, drained and chopped to ½" chunks (optional)

Finish

- 1 tablespoon lime juice (more if compensating)
- 1 handful fresh cilantro, chopped
- ½ cup grape tomatoes, halved, or 2 plum tomatoes coarsely chopped (optional)

Tools

- 1 large pot, at least 3 quarts
- Knife-cutting board

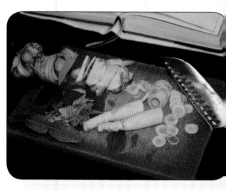

asian

Step 2: Make Broth

Combine all broth ingredients (coconut milk, stock, salt, sugar, shallots/garlic, coriander, galanga, lemongrass, kaffir lime leaves, chili sauce), bring to a low boil, and simmer for at least 15 minutes.

Step 3: Strain Broth

Pour through a sieve/strainer to remove chunks, and return the broth to your big pot. You can rescue a few items from the strainer, mince them, and return them to the pot if you like—I usually don't bother. You can usually smoosh more tasty liquid out of the chunks if you try, so give them a stiff squeeze.

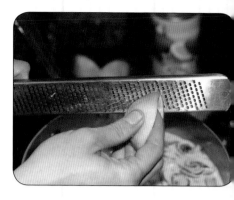

Step 5: Finish and Serve

Add the cilantro and tomatoes. Taste—the soup should be fragrant, with a rich (fatty) taste, and a mix of sweet, sour/salty flavors in the broth. You can tweak the latter with more sugar (sweet), lime juice (sour), or soy sauce (salty and tangy). Serve hot. This soup keeps beautifully, and will taste even better the next day after the flavors mingle overnight. You may want to hit it with a bit more fresh lime after reheating, though, just to keep it zippy.

Step 4: Add Chunks

Chop tofu, mushrooms, and baby corn and add to pot with broth. Add soy sauce and lime zest if using. Simmer lightly until the tofu is cooked.

asian

Fried Tofu
By jessyratfink
(http://www.instructables.com/ id/fried-tofu/)

Fried tofu is the only way I've been able to get perfect tofu stir-fries, amazing pad Thai, and even a really excellent Italian-herb-breaded tofu awesomeness. Fried tofu is even super yummy all by itself—and I own up to making it and then dipping it in buffalo sauce.

While it might seem like it'll be tricky or take too much time, it's really quite simple when you do it right, and those few extra minutes of frying the tofu are worth the crispy exterior and creamy inside. Plus, you don't use very much oil for the frying, which is excellent, and you can use the same oil to cook veggies after!

I've been trying to perfect fried tofu for about six months now, and I am utterly in love with the way I'm doing it currently. There are a few important things to remember when making fried tofu, but when you get the process down, it's nearly foolproof!

Step 1: What You'll Need
- 1 package firm/extra firm tofu
- A few tablespoons canola/vegetable oil
- Salt
- Paper towels or lintless towels of some sort

I've done this with medium tofu bu it didn't work quite as well—it break apart much easier. You can also use a different sort of oil if you like, as long as it has a high smoke point! You'll need the towels for drying the tofu. I've used cloth towels before and it works great Just make sure whatever you're using won't leave part of itself on the tofu.

Step 2: Drain and Press the Tofu
Open the tofu package and drain the tofu well. Now, there are two way to go about pressing it: Press it in one big block (will need 15 to 20 minutes) or cut it and then press it (best for when you're trying to get food on the table quickly).

Before you do either of these, pu a couple paper towels down on the surface the tofu will be sitting and then sprinkle the tofu with salt. The sal is essential—it will help pull the moisture out of the tofu and season it.

If you're pressing it as a block: lay down a couple sheets of paper towels put down the tofu, sprinkle with salt and cover it with a couple more pape towels. Put a plate with something heavy on it on top. (Not too heavy though— anything heavier than a 14-ounce can s too much. I've had tofu burst. True tory.) I like to use a ramekin. Leave for t least 15 minutes and then blot the ofu dry with more paper towels.

If you're cutting then pressing: cut he tofu to the size you like. Lay it down nto paper towels and sprinkle with salt. Then cover with more paper towels and press down gently with the palm of your hand. Press all over until the top layer of paper towels begins to get wet. Now let his sit for a few minutes. If you have a cutting board or something similar that vill cover the cut up tofu, feel free to use hat to press it.

Step 3: Use the Pressing Time as a Prep Break!

I cut up lots of veggies and started a stir fry sauce while the tofu was finishing.

asian

89

Step 4: Frying!

Add a few tablespoons of oil to a pan (nonstick is best, but I've done this in stainless steel too). Heat the oil over medium-high heat until it shimmers. I tend to go with seven on my gas stove. At this point, make sure that your tofu is *really* dry. Blot it again with paper towels. If it's wet, your kitchen will get dangerous very fast.

Add the tofu to the pan and let it cook on the first side for about three minutes. Don't overcrowd the pan or it won't fry, it'll steam instead! When you see that the bottom of the sides are nice and brown it's time to flip (see the second photo for what this should look like).

Once it flips, give it another 2 to 3 minutes. The tofu should be nice and golden brown and smell slightly nutty when done! Keep in mind that cooking times will vary depending on your heat, so just be patient and keep checking the color. When the tofu is done, set it aside and let the oil drain on paper towels. Make sure to not fry it too much—if the tofu goes a darker brown color it's going to be crunchy all the way through and you'll miss out on the lovely creamy bits inside.

asian

Step 5: Additional Recommendations

On this tofu frying day I made a veggie stir fry to go with it and a sauce. If you have time when cooking with tofu, it's always best to fry it and then let it simmer in a sauce. It'll be much more flavorful.

I've also coated the tofu in beaten egg and cornstarch, but it came out quite egg-y and it wasn't worth the extra work. Same goes for egg and soy sauce. Though I do recommend marinating the tofu and then frying—that's turned out quite well. Soy sauce, ginger, garlic, and sesame oil was also quite yummy.

asian

Tender Seitan Slices in Herbed Gravy

By SLCVeganista
(http://www.instructables
.com/id/Tender-Seitan-Slices-In-
Herbed-Gravy/)

Turkeys aren't very thankful when it comes to Thanksgiving due to the fact that they all know they are going to be the main course in most households across North America. As a longtime dedicated vegan, I am always looking for main course alternatives to meat, poultry, and fish.

Seitan (pronounced say-tahn) is not to be confused with Satan, which is also known as the Devil. Seitan isn't evil; it's just misunderstood.

Seitan has been around for centuries, but for the average con-sumer, it seems it is only now a new revelation. Seitan is also known as Meat of Wheat, as it is made using vital wheat gluten. Making your own seitan isn't as complicated as most people assume it is. It can take a long time, if you make it completely from scratch (which involves isolating the wheat gluten on your own by starting with 8 cups of white flour and 8 cups of whole wheat flour mixed with water to form a dough and then washing and rinsing the dough until all the water runs clear, which can take several hours.)

Over the years, I have tried many, many seitan recipes and all of them fell short somehow, so I developed this recipe using a lot of trial and error. Now I think it has reached perfection, as well as an award-winning status. Lucky for all of you, there are shortcuts that make

this very easy to make. The key to this recipe is the gravy. If your gravy is good, your seitan will also taste good.

We all like easy and uncomplicated recipes, especially during the hectic holiday season when time always runs out at the most inopportune moments.

Step 1: Ingredients and Equipment

Ingredients

- 3 cups vital wheat gluten flour (I use Bob's Red Mill, but use whatever you can find)
- 1 15-ounce can organic garbanzo beans, drained and rinsed (or dried garbanzo beans that have been fully cooked, drained and rinsed)
- 2 cups herbed gravy

Equipment

- Heavy-duty aluminum foil
- Food processor with an S-blade
- Steamer (You can use a big pot with a lid and a colander instead if that is all you have.)
- Colander
- Measuring cups
- Can opener (if you are using canned garbanzo beans)
- Saucepan
- Spoon or spatula for stirring

Herbed Gravy

ingredients

- ¼ cup vegan margarine (I use Earth Balance Original, either Buttery Spread or Buttery Sticks)
- ½ cup fresh minced herbs of choice (rosemary, oregano, thyme, sage, etc.) 2 tablespoons dried herbs of choice (usually a mixture of Organic Poultry Seasoning and Kirkland Organic No Salt Seasoning from Costco)
- 2 vegan chicken-style bouillon cubes (I use No-Chicken Bouillon Cubes from Edward & Sons)
- 4 cups plain unsweetened nondairy milk (I use almond milk)
- ¼ cup tapioca flour (Bob's Red Mill or other brand)
- 1–2 teaspoons garlic granules or powder
- 1–2 teaspoons onion powder or flakes
- Salt and pepper to taste (Note: Bouillon cubes are salty, so you probably won't need to add any additional salt.)

Step 2: Make Gravy

Melt margarine/heat oil in a saucepan on low heat. Add minced herbs. Dissolve corn starch/tapioca starch/flour in 3 cups cold, plain, unsweetened almond or other nondairy milk. Add to saucepan, along with vegan bouillon cube dissolved in water, garlic, and onion powder and salt and pepper if desired. Stir continuously on medium heat until gravy thickens. Use to make tender seitan slices with herbed gravy.

Step 3: Mix Seitan

Now that you have the recipe, let's get started! You will want to make the gravy first. Once made, set it aside and allow to cool. It can be warm, but if it is too hot, you will burn your hands when trying to knead the seitan. Set up your food processor with the S-blade. Prepare garbanzo beans by draining and rinsing off with cool water in a colander. Add garbanzo beans to the food processor bowl and pulse for 30 to 45 seconds, or until they are well chopped (but not pureed). Add cooled gravy to pulsed garbanzo beans. Pulse again for 30 to 45 seconds or until well blended.

Slowly add vital wheat gluten flour to the food processor a cup at a time. You know it's done when it starts to form a ball of soft, stretchy, slightly shiny dough. Remove from food processor and knead for 3 to 5 minutes or until smoothed out. Cover and allow to rest 30 minutes.

asian

Step 4: Steam Seitan

Meanwhile, start a pot of water to boil or set up a steamer. Break into four smaller balls of dough and roll out into logs. Wrap tightly in foil and steam seitan for 1 hour and 15 minutes.

Note: Depending on your steamer size, you may not be able to fit all of them in there at once. That's okay, but make sure all your raw seitan is wrapped in foil until ready to be steamed. It is best to steam it as soon as possible, because it doesn't turn out as well if you wait more than a couple of hours.

asian

Step 5: Slice Seitan

Carefully remove foil packet from steam, unwrap, and allow to cool slightly before slicing. After being steamed and sliced, place slices in a lightly greased baking dish, completely cover slices with vegan herbed gravy, then cover dish with foil and bake at 350°F for 60 to 90 minutes. Serve alongside other veganized Thanksgiving foods (such as mashed potatoes, festive cranberry relish, candied yams, wild rice stuffing, and, if you are not stuffed yet, gluten-free vegan pumpkin or pecan pie.

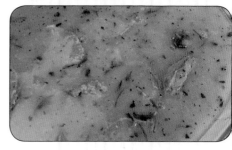

asian

How to Make Seitan

By ChrysN
(http://www.instructables.com/
id/How-To-Make-Seitan-1/)

Equipment

- Measuring cups and spoons
- Large bowl
- Spoon for stirring
- Sifter
- Large cooking pot

Seitan or wheat gluten (wheat-meat) is a great meat alternative for vegetarians. As vegetarians know, combining legumes and grains such as humus and pita, rice and beans, or peanut butter on bread creates a complete protein (provides all the essential amino acids); this seitan recipe does the same by using soy and corn flour with the wheat gluten.

Step 1: Ingredients and Equipment

Ingredients

- ¼ cup flour
- ¼ cup corn flour (or fine grind corn meal)
- ¼ cup soy flour
- 1½ cup vital wheat gluten*
- ½ teaspoon salt
- ½ teaspoon baking powder
- 1½ cups vegetable stock**
- Another 2 quarts vegetable stock**

---

*Vital wheat gluten or wheat gluten can be found in regular grocery stores and health food stores.

**The vegetable stock gives the seitan its flavor; feel free to add other spices or seasoning to your taste ie; garlic, soy sauce, tamari, etc.

Step 2

Measure and sift the flours into a large bowl.

Step 3

Add the salt and baking powder, then mix the dry ingredients.

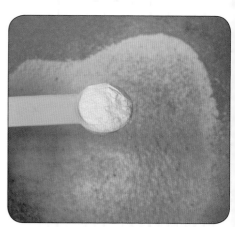

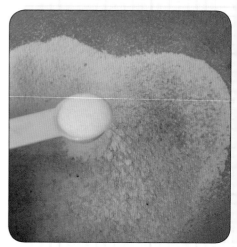

Step 4

Add the vegetable stock and mix well with a spoon.

Step 6

Knead again for about a minute and let rest for 10 minutes.

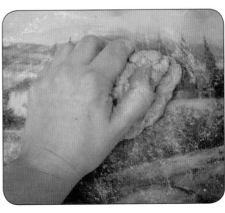

Step 5

Knead and let rest for 20 minutes.

asian

Step 7: Knead and Slice

Knead again, this time putting pressure in the centre of the dough so that it forms a ring. Cut apart the ring. Then slice about 1-centimeter-thick pieces.

Step 8: Cook Seitan

Bring the 2 quarts of vegetable stock to a boil and add the slices of dough. Stir occasionally so that they don't stick together. Turn the heat down and let simmer for 20 minutes. After 20 minutes, remove pieces from the pot and place on a plate to cool.

asian

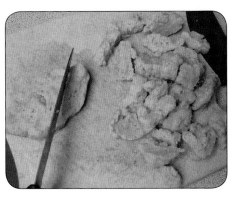

Step 9: Finished Seitan

Seitan is best sautéed before eaten. It's yummy in stir-fries and also in fajitas. Seitan can be stored "as is" in the freezer. I usually divide the pieces up into meal size portions and store them in freezers bags.

101

Roasted Eggplant with Garlic

By canida
(http://www.instructables.com/
id/Roasted-Eggplant-with-
Garlic/)

A great way to cook eggplant with minimal prep time.

Ingredients
- As much eggplant as you want
- Garlic (fresh or pre-chopped)
- Olive oil/canola oil
- Fresh pepper
- Cajun spice or salt

Optional Ingredients
- Scallions
- Parsley
- Garlic-chili powder
- Cumin
- Oregano
- Rosemary
- Any other spices you like

Step 1: Prepare Eggplant

Find yourself some nice Chinese or Japanese eggplant. These are the long skinny varieties, easily distinguishable from the globular Italian eggplant. Do not attempt to use Italian eggplant for this dish—the skin is too thick and the flesh isn't as sweet. Wash the eggplant, trim off the caps, halve lengthwise, and place them in a greased baking dish. I generally use spray canola oil and give the cut surfaces of the eggplant another spray to keep them moist in baking.

Step 2: Season

Chop a big pile of garlic, or use a jar of the pre-chopped stuff. Garlic salt really won't cut it. Sprinkle the chopped garlic over the eggplant to your preferred density, then drizzle the eggplant with a bit of olive oil. Grind fresh pepper over the top, and sprinkle with Cajun spice and/or a bit of salt. Optional additions: scallions, parsley, etc. can be chopped in with garlic-chili powder, cumin, oregano, rosemary, or the spice/herb of your choice to sprinkle on top.

Step 4: Serve

You can serve these warm or at room temperature—it's all good. They make great appetizers when cut into segments and served at room temperature, and of course make a lovely vegetarian side dish for those upcoming family gatherings.

Step 3: Roast

Put the pan in a 350°F oven for about 30 to 45 minutes. The eggplant will thin and curl on itself a bit, and the garlic will become a crisp and nutty brown on top. At this point you can remove the eggplant and eat them directly, but I prefer to shut off the oven and let them slowly cool while I go for a bike ride. This extra hour sitting at low temperature dries the eggplant out a bit more, concentrating and mellowing the flavors.

asian

Section 4
American

Effortless Chili for Cold Days

By AngryRedhead
(www.instructables.com/id/
Effortless-Chili-for-Cold-Days/)

Valentine's Day occurs during the oldest part of the year for those of us who live in the Northern Hemisphere. Here in Central Texas, winter is also the wettest part of the year which makes for pretty gross weather, especially because it typically doesn't get cold enough for snow. When it's cold and wet outside, there's not a whole lot that makes me want to go out. I don't want to put on a fancy dress and fancy shoes and eat fancy food. I much prefer snuggling up with my significant other and a large steamy bowl of comfort. He prefers that, too.

This Instructable shows how to make chili with almost no effort whatsoever. It's tasty, warm, and full of lycopene and other healthy stuff, and it's been tested and proven. It's also inexpensive ($7–$14 for a large pot's worth), so you can buy your Valentine that prized Nepenthes pitcher plant she's been wanting for the past fourteen months . . . just saying.

So grab a bowl, a blanket, and your sweetie, and cozy up in front of a fire for some good V-Day lovin'.

Step 1: Ingredients
- 1 onion (diced)
- 3–5 cloves of garlic (minced)
- 2 large cans whole peeled tomatoes
- 1 large can crushed tomatoes
- 3 regular cans of red kidney beans
- 3 tablespoons of olive oil
- 2–4 tablespoons of chili powder
- Salt

american

Optional:
- Cooked ground beef/turkey
- Rehydrated Textured Vegetable Protein (TVP)
- Cottage cheese or sour cream
- Chives
- Grated cheddar cheese
- Croutons
- Bread with a nice crust
- Grilled cheese sandwich
- Tabasco sauce

Note: When I worked at a small nonprofit, we would have "Slow Cooker Fridays," and this was a favorite meal to make. The ingredients were divided up.
- Onions, garlic, and olive oil
- Tomatoes
- Kidney beans
- Bread, croutons, cheese, etc.

I usually brought the chili powder, and there was already salt in the kitchen. If you work in a small office, I highly recommend trying this out with your coworkers. Freshly cooked food is such a relief, and it removes a bit of tension and stress in the office.

Tip for Mincing Garlic
- Place the garlic clove under the flat portion of the knife and hit the knife quickly with the butt of your hand.
- Remove the skin of the clove.
- Return clove under the flat portion of the knife and hit the knife with the butt of your hand until the clove is smashed.
- Run the knife through the smashed clove until it's fully minced.

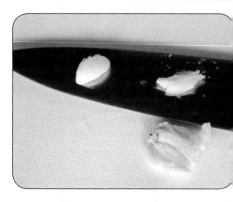

Step 2: Microwave Garlic and Onion

Microwave the diced onion and minced garlic until the onion is semi-translucent. Note: I microwaved this batch for 3½ minutes at 70 percent power.

american

Step 3: Pour and Cook

Add all the ingredients to the slow cooker, including the liquids in the cans. Note: If you want meat or TVP, add it at this point. Stir. Cook on low for 3 to 5 hours. Serve and garnish.

american

Portobello Mushroom with Grilled Feta Burger

By ChrysN
(http://www.instructables.com/
id/Portobello-Mushroom-with-
Grilled-Feta-Burger/)

Here is a great meatless burger that even non-vegetarians will enjoy. This burger is first marinated with balsamic vinegar, basil, rosemary, and garlic and grilled. Then a slice of grilled feta cheese is placed on top to make this burger really flavorful.

Portobello (also spelled portabella or portabello) mushrooms are brown crimini mushrooms left to grow to reach four to 6 inches in diameter. Like other mushrooms they absorb flavor from marinade really well.

Step 1: Ingredients and Equipment

Ingredients
- Portobello mushroom caps (Try to find caps about the same size as you bun—there will be a bit of shrinkage when cooked.)
- Feta cheese (not the little cubes packed in oil but a block of the cheese)
- Hamburger bun
- Toppings for your bun such as mayo, lettuce, tomatoes, onions, whatever you wish

Marinade (this is for two servings)
- 2 tablespoon balsamic vinegar
- 2–3 teaspoons olive oil
- ½ teaspoon dried basil
- ½ teaspoon dried oregano
- 1½ teaspoons minced garlic
- Salt and pepper to taste (you don't need to add very much salt since feta cheese can be quite salty)

Equipment
- Grill or barbeque
- Cutting board
- Knife
- Measuring spoons
- Spatula
- Basting brush
- Aluminum foil or parchment paper
- Shallow bowl
- Spoon

Step 2: Preparation ahead of Time

Clean mushroom caps with a nylon brush (mushroom scrubber). If you don't have one, wipe the tops with a damp cloth. Cut off stem with knife.

To a shallow bowl, add:

- 2 tablespoons balsamic vinegar
- ½ teaspoon of each of dried basil and dried rosemary
- 1½ teaspoons garlic
- 2–3 teaspoons olive oil
- Salt and pepper to taste

Stir to mix. Place mushroom in bowl for a minimum of 15 minutes to marinate, flipping the mushroom over at least twice. As you can see from my pictures, the mushroom is not entirely submersed in the marinade; that is why it's important to flip it over. I usually marinade my mushrooms an hour or two before I start making dinner. Note: After marinating the mushroom, do not throw out the marinade—you will need it later.

american

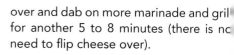

over and dab on more marinade and grill for another 5 to 8 minutes (there is no need to flip cheese over).

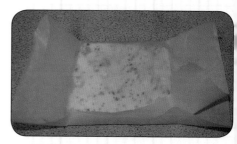

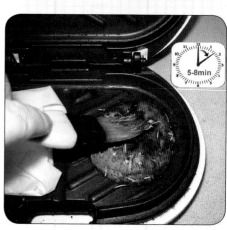

Step 3: Grill Mushroom and Cheese

Preheat grill or BBQ. Cut a slice of cheese, not too thin. Place on parchment paper or aluminum foil and wrap tightly. If you are using a barbeque, aluminum foil is probably better.

Start grilling. Place mushroom and packet with cheese on grill. They conveniently take about the same amount of time to cook. Dab some left over marinade on mushroom with basting brush. Grill for about 5 to 8 minutes. The longer the mushroom is cooked, the meatier (in terms of texture) it gets. Flip

112

Step 5: Putting It All Together

Remove mushroom from grill and place on bun. Remove cheese packet from grill, unwrap (careful, it's hot!), and place on burger. Add top of bun and serve with your favorite side dishes. Enjoy!

Step 4: Prepare Bun

While your mushroom and cheese are grilling, you can prepare your bun and toppings. You can toast the bun and add a spread like mayonnaise, butter, margarine, or cream cheese (which is what I used). Add your vegetables (lettuce, sprouts, tomatoes, onions, pickles, pepper, or whatever suits your fancy).

american

american

114

Step 3: Serving

Serve the chili in a bowl with some cornbread or toast by the side and some cheddar or parmesan cheese sprinkled on top. This chili is a very nutritious meal, and doesn't necessarily require any other side dishes.

Vegetarian Split Pea Soup

By cnixon
(http://www.instructables.com/
id/Vegetarian-Split-Pea-Soup/)

This stew is a family favorite. Normally, split pea soup is flavored with ham hocks or some other non-vegetarian ingredient, but this recipe is totally vegetarian and can be vegan if the yogurt is left out. An added benefit: this is a one dish meal! The peas are full of fiber and protein, and the veggies and rice make for a well-balanced meal. Enjoy!

Step 1: Get Ready

First, dress up in an outfit that inspires you to cook. This recipe provides four large servings (as the only dish) or up to eight smaller servings as a side dish.

For the Stew
- 1½ cups split peas
- 1 cup onions, coarsely chopped
- 8 cloves garlic
- 4 cups vegetable broth
- 2 tablespoons olive oil
- 8 oz spinach, stemmed
- ½ cup finely chopped flat leaf parsley
- ½ cup finely chopped cilantro
- 4 large tomatoes or 1 cup cherry tomatoes
- 1 tablespoon fresh dill
- Pepper flakes to taste (about 2 teaspoons)
- Salt and pepper to taste

For the Rice
- 1½ cups basmati rice
- 3 cups water
  Use plain low-fat yogurt as a garnish.

Step 2: Cook Onions and Garlic

Heat the oil in a large saucepan. Chop the garlic and the onions* and add to the oil. Sauté on medium heat until the onions are translucent. Add 3 cups of vegetable broth and bring to a boil. Add the split peas. Let simmer for 50 minutes.

*Tip: Refrigerate the onions before you chop them so they don't irritate your eyes and mess up your make-up!

Step 3: Put on the Rice

After 30 minutes, put on the rice. Boil 3 cups water, then add rice and a dash of salt. Cover and let simmer for 20 minutes.

Step 4: Chop Everything

Wash and stem the spinach. It will cook down in the stew, so there's no need to chop it unless the leaves are particularly big. Chop the dill, tomatoes, and parsley. Add into the stew in the last 15 minutes (35 minutes after adding the split peas). Stir occasionally to ensure even cooking.

Step 5: Almost Done

After 50 minutes, add salt, pepper, and pepper flakes to taste. I personally like my stew with slices of French bread, but it's good on its own, too.

american

119

Step 6: Enjoy!

Serve rice, stew, and yogurt ir bowls, pour yourself a glass of wine (o beverage of your choice), and enjoy!

american

Vegetarian Mushroom Gravy

By jforbess
(http://www.instructables.com/
id/Vegetarian-Mushroom-Gravy/)

Even vegetarians love the mashed
potatoes part of Thanksgiving, but what
re mashed potatoes without gravy?
hrough trial and error, I've learned to
nake excellent mushroom gravy for my
ister the vegetarian. It's so good that I
sually put turkey gravy on the turkey
nd save my mashed potatoes for the
nushroom gravy. Plus, I have finally
earned the secret to avoiding lumpy
ravy—and lumpy sauces in general. Fat
rst!

Step 1: Ingredients and Equipment

Critical Items

- Onions (at least one)
- Mushrooms (portabella or baby bella are best)
- About 4 tablespoon butter (olive oil would probably work, but I've never tried)
- ¼ cup flour
- ½ cup sherry or marsala (other flavored liquids would work, but these have the best flavor here)
- 2–4 cups liquid (ideally vegetable broth)

Extra Bonus Items

- Garlic (as much as you like)
- Thyme, dried or fresh
- Paprika
- Fresh parsley

You'll need two pans. First you sauté
nions, garlic, and mushrooms in one.
hen make the roux in the second. Then
dd the first pan to the second pan.

Step 2: Chopping

Since this is a gravy, I chop the
ingredients finely. Minced onions,
minced garlic, thinly sliced mushrooms.
I almost never chop things finely, but it's
worth it. The liquids cook out faster and
the gravy is smoother.

american

121

Step 3: Sautéing

You can throw your ingredients in, fry 'em up without thinking, and have something that works, or you can pay attention, and have something great.

Fry the onions in a little butter or olive oil on high to medium high heat. We want really nice brown bits to give the gravy that great roasted taste. Obviously avoid burning them. Onions have quite a bit of liquid inside them, so they can take a pretty high heat, but once they start turning brown, pay more attention and stir more often to minimize the chance of burning. Add the garlic when the onions are close to done. Garlic burns easily on high heat, so this is when you want to turn down the heat to medium or medium low. Now, add the mushrooms. They'll have a decent amount of liquid in them from the washing, so we want to cook them slowly to draw it out nicely for the sauce. This time I ended up adding one box of mushrooms first, then chopping and adding the second. This led to a nice gradation from totally cooked mushroom bits to fairly solid mushroom slices. If I weren't so lazy, I might have cooked them longer for a smoother gravy, but a few slices are nice too.

After the mushrooms have cooked down a little, add the thyme and paprika. I tend to sprinkle, mix, smell, or taste, and repeat the process until I'm happy. I'm horrible at estimating times for these steps, and it's more important to get it to the right doneness than check the time. But the onions might take 10 minutes, the garlic may take 1 minute, and the mushrooms another 10 minutes. However, while the mushrooms are cooking, you can start the roux. (And if the mushrooms are done before the roux, you can take them off the heat until you're ready for them, or vice versa.)

american

and flour. It just happens to be liquid instead of solid.

tep 4: Roux—the Basis of :uropean Sauciness

I don't know much about classic auces, but I have learned the key to ood gravy: mix the fat with the flour rst. Then cook it. Then add the liquid. o, equal parts fat and flour. For this ecipe, about 4 tablespoons of butter nd ¼ cup flour. (Yes, those are equivalent mounts. Silly Imperial system.) Melt the utter in a new pan (everything will end p in this pan at the end, so it should be easonably big) over medium heat. Mix the flour. It'll bubble oddly. It looks nd smells like Playdoh. Kind of gross, ght?

Keep stirring. And stirring. And tirring. You don't want to burn it, but ou do want to brown it. So medium eat is good. Lots of stirring. Thick-ottomed pans are better here for an ven heat. I can usually tell that my roux ready from the smell more than the olor. It goes from smelling like Playdoh smelling like baked pie crust. And asically, that's what it is: cooked butter

Step 5: Deglazing the Mushrooms

Once you've got the roux ready to go, you should deglaze the mushrooms. Deglazing is the point at which you use a liquid to melt those tasty brown bits (fond) off the sides of the pan. I just sprinkle as much sherry as I need, which is probably between ½ and ¼ of a cup. All of the alcohol cooks off, so we're just doing it for the rich flavors. If you don't have sherry on hand, you could use Marsala wine, vermouth, or red or white wine. I think at one point I used a mix of

american

apple cider vinegar and water, but that was a long time ago. Once the fond is mixed into the liquid, you're ready to add this to the roux.

coated with thick gravy? Yum. This is where you could mix in some minced fresh parsley.

Step 6: Mixing It All Together

Pour the mushroom bits into the roux. Stir a lot. It'll foam up, but just keep stirring and pouring. The sauce should be thick and glossy. It'll probably be too thick. This is when you add vegetable broth or water to thin it out. If it's really thick, don't just add veggie broth—it's too salty. Add water too. If you're frugal like my Depression-raised grandmother, you'll add the potato water from your mashed potatoes. Theoretically it has lots of vitamins, and it's already hot. See how the sides of the pan are nicely

Vegetarian Turkey

By frenzy
(http://www.instructables.com/
id/Vegetarian-Turkey/)

Want a vegetarian turkey you can serve on Thanksgiving that's like a tofurkey? Want to make it yourself?

Then this turkey is for you! This recipe uses vital wheat gluten to get a nice meaty texture and, along with some spices and a rice stuffing, even the non-veggies will say "Yum!"

Step 1: Ingredients

- 2 cups of vital wheat gluten
- 2 cups of veggie broth
- 3 tablespoons rosemary
- 3 tablespoons thyme
- 1 tablespoon seasoned salt (or garlic powder, onion powder, etc.)
- 1 bag of wild rice (about 2 cups)

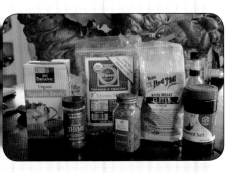

Step 2: Cook Rice

First you want to cook the wild rice in a rice cooker. If you don't have a rice cooker, get creative with the stove!

Step 3: Mix Dry Ingredients

Mix the spices and the wheat gluten together until well mixed. Add more spices as you want.

Step 5: Stuff the Gluten

Next you want to get your stuffing into the gluten. For this we are using cooked rice. You could use anything else, of course, but I feel the rice adds a healthy bit to this dish.

Step 4: Add Broth and Knead

Next add the broth to the dry mix. Knead it around until it's all wet.

Step 6: Boil the Loafs

Next start some broth of soy sauce and molasses (2 tablespoons of each) in about 6 cups of water and bring to a boil. Place your loaf in the water and let simmer for around an hour. They will grow and get puffy.

bake it. Otherwise, it will take you about an hour to bake the loaf. Drizzle the loaf with olive oil and add some root veggies around it if you wish. Bake for about an hour or until crisp at 350°F.

Step 8: Serve

And that's about it. The loaf is done after baking. Serve with regular Thanksgiving fixin's like gravy, mashed potatoes, and cranberry sauce.

Step 7: Bake the Loaf

Next you want to bake the loaf. At this point you could freeze it and wait to

american

127

Easy Bean Burgers

By jessyratfink
(http://www.instructables.com/
id/Easy-Bean-Burgers/)

These bean burgers are super easy and very quick to make—not to mention you can add in so many things to suit your tastes! This is just a base recipe, so go wild.

These take about 30–45 minutes to make, and have a very short ingredient list. One can of beans can make four burgers!

Step 1: Ingredients and Equipment

Ingredients

- 1 14-ounce can OR 2 cups beans of your choice (I'm using chickpeas and black beans)
- 1 medium onion, cut into large chunks
- ½ cup rolled oats (not instant)
- 1 tablespoon spice of your choice (I'm using chili powder in the black beans, cumin in the chickpeas)
- Salt and pepper to taste
- 1 egg
- Oil for cooking (olive or canola)

Equipment

- Large pan for frying
- Food processor
- Spatulas, forks, etc.
- Cutting boards

Step 2: Assemble the Bean Mixture

Get out your food processor—if you have one that's 4 cups or more, feel free to dump everything in. If you're working with a little tiny one like me, first mix everything together in a bowl and do it in two batches.

Open your can of beans and drain it, reserving the liquid just in case. (I've not had to use it, but who knows!) Cut your onion into chunks. Combine the beans, ½ cup of oats, spices, the egg, onion, salt, and pepper in your bowl and mix together. The first picture is chickpeas with cumin, the second picture is black beans with chili powder.

Step 3: Pulse, Pulse, Pulse

Once you get a reasonable amount of the mixture into your food processor, you'll start to pulse. Pulse a few times, take the top off, scrape down the sides, repeat. You only want to do this until things start to break down—but you don't want things to get pureed. It still needs to be slightly chunky and have good body. Also, don't add any liquid at all if you can help it. The mixture is wet enough as-is and should mix up on its own. But if for some odd reason your food processor starts smoking and screaming, add a tablespoon or so of liquid. The last picture shows you what you should end up with—a good, firm, chunky consistency.

What to do if it gets too thin or you got too excited while pulsing: Put a tablespoon or two of extra oats in your second batch if you have a small food processor, or just empty everything but

american

129

a small amount of the mixture and add in the oats.

Step 4: Form the Patties

Wet your hands and shake off any excess. Wet hands are especially important for this bit—otherwise you just get gloppy bean hands, and no one wants that. I had the best luck making four patties out of the mixture, but you can make up to six. Divide the mixture into equal parts, roll into balls, and then flatten carefully into patties. I found it was easiest to do this on a big flexible cutting board that I could carry around with me. I'd just make them into balls and then flatten them while they were on the board. Don't make them too thin or they become very hard to pick back up and they'll start to break. And don't press too hard into the surface you're working on either, or they'll stick like crazy!

Step 5: Cooking the Patties

Now the best part! Heat a pan over medium heat with your oil of choice. Once the oil is nice and hot, coax the patties off your work station (keep in mind you can reshape them a little in the pan if you need to) and into the pan. Don't overcrowd them, though—two to three patties is the maximum. If they're touching too much, they will not get crispy because they'll just steam.

Cook for five minutes on one side, flip, and cook for an additional five minutes. Make sure to move them around a little during this time—stove tops and pans can be finicky, and you don't want one to get burnt while the other stays golden brown. And if a patty breaks during flipping, no worries, just craft yourself a falafel-esque bite and consider that your tip for cooking.

Step 6: Toppings and Other Ideas

Top these as you would any other burger. I suspect almost anything would be good on them. The black bean ones were my favorite, but the chickpea ones are also quite good. I can't wait to try additional combinations and I'm looking

american

131

forward to trying more veggies and fresh herbs in there! The original recipe came from one of the kings of cooking, Mark Bittman.

Eggplant Bacon

By shesparticular
(http://www.instructables.com/
id/Eggplant-Bacon/)

Bacon is one of the most delicious foods ever but one that vegetarians, vegans, and other folks with dietary restrictions are sure to miss at breakfast time (and lunch, and dinner, and snacks). With a few simple ingredients, you can make a yummy bacon-proxy sure to please all your brunch guests—even pork-aholics.

Step 1: You'll Need

Software

- A few small eggplants (Japanese or Italian work best; small ones are preferred since they have fewer or no seeds)
- Bacon salt (I like to use the maple or natural, but it's up to you.) (If you don't have bacon salt or don't have access to it, you can try a mix of salt, pepper, brown sugar, and paprika and maybe a little onion and garlic powder.)
- Oil for frying (vegetable or canola works well)

Hardware

- A mandolin for slicing (if you don't have one, you can use a very sharp knife)
- A medium-sized mixing bowl and a sheet pan with some type of cooling/straining rack over it (sheet pan method is not required, but is recommended)
- Large cast iron skillet
- Kitchen tongs
- Paper towels (brown paper bags can also be used)

Step 2: Prep Your 'Plants

Wash your eggplants well. Peel if desired (leaving the peel on results in crisper slices later. Using the mandolin (or knife,) slice approximately 1/8-inch-thick pieces. Make sure to use the finger guard and be very careful so you don't cut yourself! Put the slices into the mixing bowl and sprinkle in bacon salt (you'll need a lot). Toss the slices around with your fingers until all slices are coated on both sides. You can keep

american

133

the slices in this bowl or transfer them to the draining rack placed over the sheet pan (if using). Allow to sit for at least 30 minutes to allow the bitter fluid to drain from the eggplant.

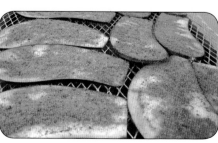

Step 3: Fry 'Em Up

Pour approximately 1 inch of oil into your cast iron pan and heat over medium-high heat. Once the oil is nice and hot, gently wipe off the extra liquid (and some of the bacon salt) from each eggplant slice, add slices one at a time to the oil. Be very careful! The high water content in the eggplant slices will make the oil splatter a lot!

Fry until crispy and lightly browned all over (or more brown if you like your bacon extra crispy). Remove from pan using tongs and place on a layer of paper towels or brown paper bags to wick away the excess oil. Enjoy as is, or make yourself a delicious ELT (eggplant, lettuce, and tomato) sandwich!

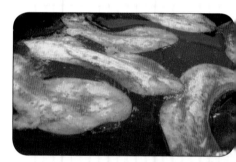

Aubergines (Eggplants) with Walnut Paste Stuffing

By Vika84
(http://www.instructables.com/
id/Aubergines-eggplants-with-
walnut-paste-stuffing/)

This is a very delicious snack that can be used as a starter, too. It's quick and easy to make. I would like to add that pomegranate seeds give a lovely taste to this snack but I did not have any when I was making this one. If you decide to make this snack one day and manage to get pomegranate seeds, then mix them into the walnut paste. You can also sprinkle the pomegranate seeds over the dish for lovely decoration, which will look like pink pearls on the plate!

Step 1: Walnut Paste

Ingredients
- 200 grams of walnuts (oily walnuts preferable—not too dry)
- Bunch of fresh coriander
- Half of a medium onion
- 2 or 3 medium garlic cloves
- 1 teaspoon of chilli
- 1 teaspoon of coriander powder
- Salt by taste
- About 200 milliliters of water

Mince (with a mincer or food processor) walnuts, finely chopped coriander, garlic, and finely chopped onion. Add coriander powder, chilli, and salt to the minced mixture. Mix it well with the spoon and start adding some water to it, so the mixture will become like a whiting paste. Paste is ready! As simple as that!

135

Step 2: Preparation of Aubergines

Small aubergines are the best! If you cannot get small aubergines, then try to fine big long ones. Easy way to prepare them is to cut the top ends off, cut them in half, and stick them into the microwave for 2 minutes to start with. In order to check if aubergines are ready, prick them with a knife in couple of places. If the insides of the aubergines are soft, they are ready; if they are hard, then you need to put them into the microwave for a bit longer (till they get soft).

When the aubergines are nice and soft, take them out from the microwave and cool them down a bit. When the aubergines are cool enough to touch, take a spoon and scoop the insides out. Finely cut these insides and mix them with the walnut paste.

american

136

Step 4: Decoration and Presentation of the Dish

- Piping bag for the mayo
- Salad leaves
- Dill or cress
- Mayo
- Tomatoes
- Pomegranate is great for sprinkling

Put salad leaves on the plate and spread the stuffed aubergine pieces on them, decorate the plate with tomatoes or pomegranate seeds or both, and sprinkle the dish with cress or dill weed. Enjoy!

Step 3: Putting All the Ingredients Together

Take the walnut paste and put t inside the aubergines. Roll the aubergines into an original shape (there will still be a little bit of an opening on he side of the aubergine but that's fine). Cut the aubergine into small pieces as shown on the photo (the knife should be quite sharp to make a clean cut). The snack is ready!

american

american

Vegan Beef Stroganoff

By crystalmath
(http://www.instructables.com/
id/Vegan-Beef-Stroganoff/)

This delicious dish will be sure to impress crowds from all dietary walks of life!

Step 1: Ingredients and Equipment

Ingredients

- 12 ounces (1 box) of Yves Meatless ground "beef"
- 4–5 tablespoons of Earth Balance
- 1½–2 cups Eden Blend Rice and Soymilk
- ⅓ cup Tofutti Better than Sour Cream
- ½ cup nutritional yeast
- 3 small purple onions
- 4–6 cloves of garlic
- 1 box (12 ounces) pasta
- 4 ounces of spinach
- 2–3 tablespoons olive oil

Equipment

- Garlic peeler and press
- Medium-sized knife
- Large saucepan
- Pasta pot
- Wooden or plastic-slotted spoon

A lot of these measurements are estimated—this means they can/should be altered by the cook as the cook sees fit. If you want more sauce, use more rice and soymilk. If you want it creamer, add more Better than Sour Cream. If you want more veggies, add more veggies.

I used Yves brand because it wasn't already flavored and it is a good base in general. You could probably also use Gimme Lean that comes in a tube if it's more accessible. For the margarine, I'm a big fan of Earth Balance made with Olive Oil for its light flavor. Any other variation of EB would do just fine.

The first time I cooked this dish, I used celery as my veggie weapon of choice. This time I had a bunch of spinach that needed to be eaten. I definitely encourage you to get experimental with this Instructable—add your own veggies, delete some, do whatever you want with it!

Step 2: Pasta and Prep Work

Depending on how quickly you can cut and peel garlic and onions, begin with boiling the pasta. I used penne pasta, which took about ten minutes to cook, all the while peeling garlic and slicing onions for sautéing in a large saucepan.

You want the saucepan to heat up but not to burn the garlic and onions (unless a smoky flavor is part of your objective). I recommend heating the saucepan on high for a few minutes and testing the heat by hovering your hand over the center of the saucepan. If it is too hot, reduce heat to medium or medium-low to avoid burn anything.

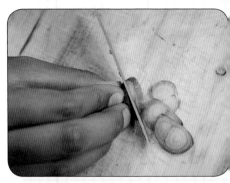

Step 3: Drain Pasta and Add "Beef"

This is where the magic happens. Once your pasta is finished cooking ("al dente" if you please—the pasta will continue to cook once it is placed in the saucepan with other ingredients) add the Earth Balance, Eden Blend Rice and Soymilk, nutritional yeast, meatless ground, and Better than Sour Cream.

The sour cream is really what makes it a stroganoff dish and not Hamburger Helper-like. It also makes the sauce creamier with a subtle taste that compliments the pasta really well. Sti

all ingredients together with a slotted spoon over medium heat. Be sure all the meatless ground breaks down and nutritional yeast is well-incorporated in your dish.

Step 4: Stop—Veggie Time

Add your veggie of choice. As someone who grew up watching *Great Chefs*, I love incorporating color into everything I create. Spinach not only adds great color and interest to the final product but is a great source of iron.

Step 5: Cover Before Serving

The basic idea is to have cooked pasta and cooked "beef," but the spinach should remain steamed at most. If the spinach is cooked too long, it may lose its flavor. So cover it up and let it sit for 5 to 7 minutes. I don't have a proper cover for this particular saucepan but a wok cover did just fine (I've used cookie sheets before and they do the trick as well).

american

141

Step 6: Get Served

The most gratifying part of cooking is tasting the result. I toasted up some vegan rye bread to accompany this delicious and cruelty-free dish. Add salt and pepper to taste if that's your thing. This dish is perfect for big dinners with lots of friends—make it to take it to a potluck or to a house dinner with house/ dorm mates. It's also a great leftover dish for days afterward.

american

Wicked Easy Bean Salad

By domestic_engineer
(http://www.instructables.com/
id/Wicked-Easy-Bean-Salad/)

This salad is really quick, really easy, and really, really yummy.

Step 1: Ingredients

- 1 can red kidney beans
- 1 can chick peas (a.k.a. garbanzo beans)
- Tomatoes
- Italian dressing (I like Ken's Light Italian. You want a dressing with a bit of spice, no Hidden Valley crap.)
- Cucumbers (optional)
- Feta cheese or mozzarella cheese (optional)
- Green peppers (optional)
- Celery, baked tofu, tuna fish, green beans . . . whatever you want

Step 2: Directions

Drain the beans (I don't rinse them). Chop up the tomatoes and peppers. Toss it all together in the big bowl. Add Italian dressing (about ¼ cup) and toss it together.

Eat and enjoy. If you put it in the fridge, the beans will absorb some of the dressing. This is a quick and easy meal. You can bring it to a pot luck/barbeque; it's also really good to take on a picnic.

american

Best Vegetarian Chicken Nuggets

By ERCBIENG
(http://www.instructables.com/
id/Best-Vegetarian-Chicken-
Nuggets/)

This is a very simple and delicious recipe for vegetarian chicken nuggets. They have a crispy crust and tender center. It only takes about 10 minutes to make and they are the best vegetarian chicken nuggets I have ever had. (That peaks volumes because I am not a vegetarian.)

Step 1: Ingredients and Equipment

Ingredients
- 1½ cup flour
- ½ tablespoon salt
- ½ cup bread crumbs
- 1 large egg
- ½ tablespoon Cayenne pepper (optional)
- 1 can of low fat Worthington scallops

Equipment
- Deep fryer
- Large bag (zip-lock)
- Can opener
- Strainer
- Large bowl

Step 2: Preparation

Turn your deep fryer on to 375°F. Open can of low fat Worthington scallops and empty some (not all) of the canning juice into the sink, leaving about 2 tablespoons in the can. Empty the can and remaining juice into your large bag. Crack your egg and empty the contents into your bag. Now for the fun part: Shake vigorously! Make sure your egg yolk is broken.

Step 3: Dry Mix

Combine all dry ingredients (flour, bread crumbs, and salt) in large bowl. Empty your scallops into the mixed bowl and stir. You can add more flour if you see bare or wet spots on the fake meat. If you like spicy chicken nuggets, you can add Cayenne pepper to your dry mix before the scallops.

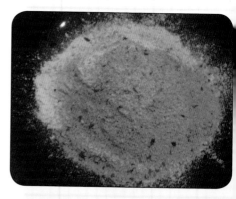

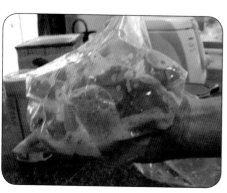

Step 4: Deep Fry

Do not crowd the "chicken" when you place it in the deep fryer or the food will not cook evenly. Cook for 4 to 5 minutes. After they are done cooking, place the chicken nuggets on a napkin on a plate to absorb excess oil. Allow the nuggets to cool for 1 minute.

Step 5: Enjoy

After cooling, serve and enjoy! One can of scallops can usually feed about four people, making about eighteen to twenty nuggets.

Other Ideas: You can cut the scallops (before shaking) into small pieces to make popcorn "chicken." You can also add a variety of spices to the dry mix to change the flavor. (Don't stray from the basic dry mix.)

american

CONVERSION TABLES

One person's inch is another person's centimeter. Instructables projects come from all over the world, so here's a handy reference guide that will help keep your project on track.

Measurement

	1 Millimeter	1 Centimeter	1 Meter	1 Inch	1 Foot	1 Yard	1 Mile	1 Kilometer
Millimeter	1	10	1,000	25.4	304.8	—	—	—
Centimeter	0.1	1	100	2.54	30.48	91.44	—	—
Meter	0.001	0.01	1	0.025	0.305	0.91	—	1,000
Inch	0.04	0.39	39.37	1	12	36	—	—
Foot	0.003	0.03	3.28	0.083	1	3	—	—
Yard	—	0.0109	1.09	0.28	033	1	—	—
Mile	—	—	—	—	—	—	1	0.62
Kilometer	—	—	1,000	—	—	—	1.609	1

Volume

	1 Milliliter	1 Liter	1 Cubic Meter	1 Tea-spoon	1 Tablespoon	1 Fluid Ounce	1 Cup	1 Pint	1 Quart	1 Gall
Milliliter	1	1,000	—	4.9	14.8	29.6	—	—	—	—
Liter	0.001	1	1,000	0.005	0.015	0.03	0.24	0.47	0.95	3.79
Cubic Meter	—	0.001	1	—	—	—	—	—	—	0.00
Teaspoon	0.2	202.9	—	1	3	6	48	—	—	—
Tablespoon	0.068	67.6	—	0.33	1	2	16	32	—	—
Fluid Ounce	0.034	33.8	—	0.167	0.5	1	8	16	32	—
Cup	0.004	4.23	—	0.02	0.0625	0.125	1	2	4	16
Pint	0.002	2.11	—	0.01	0.03	0.06	05	1	2	8
Quart	0.001	1.06	—	0.005	0.016	0.03	0.25	.05	1	4
Gallon	—	0.26	264.17	0.001	0.004	0.008	0.0625	0.125	0.25	1

Mass and Weight

	1 Gram	1 Kilogram	1 Metric Ton	1 Ounce	1 Pound	1 Short Ton
Gram	1	1,000	—	28.35	—	—
Kilogram	0.001	1	1,000	0.028	0.454	—
Metric Ton	—	0.001	1	—	—	0.907
Ounce	0.035	35.27	—	1	16	—
Pound	0.002	2.2	—	0.0625	1	2,000
Short Ton	—	0.001	1.1	—	—	1

Speed

	1 Mile per hour	1 Kilometer per hour
Miles per hour	1	0.62
Kilometers per hour	1.61	1

Temperature

	Fahrenheit (°F)	Celsius (°C)
Fahrenheit	—	(°C x 1.8) + 32
Celsius	(°F − 32) / 1.8	—